SO-EGI-779

A path from where you are to where you want to be.

What you don't see, standing in that garbage dump, is just ahead, around the corner—the heights of joy, peace, happiness, and success. You just need to believe in your unlimited potential.

Loving You is Easy, Loving Me is Hard

A Path from Pain and Despair to Self-Love and Success

Laurie Kroeger

"Whatever our path in life this book has something for everyone. We have probably all done the 'pity parties/,' the 'blame game,' and the 'I'm just not good enough' story. This book will inspire you to understand your own journey, help you to find the motivation to do something about it and feel excited about your new goals. A great work of love Laurie!! Thank you."

~ B. Gail Yearian, Lincoln, NE

"In my lifetime, I have met very few people who have proven to be not only relevant, but also inspirational. Laurie Kroeger is one of those people. She has faced and overcome many obstacles throughout the years. She uses these experiences expertly to illustrate her own journey as she struggled to take back her God-given power and become the leader of her own life.

"I was honored to be asked to read and review Loving You is Easy, Loving Me is Hard.

"The book speaks to me on many levels. Laurie is so relatable that I found myself cheering her on, while also making relevant connections to my own life and to my own struggles. I believe we all want to live life on our own terms, but most of us, including myself, really have no idea how to accomplish this ideal. Laurie's counsel, along with her approach and the

many resources she suggests are valuable tools to be utilized to finally know self-love and to become my own best friend, thus coming to a place of peace and happiness in my life. Everyone could benefit by reading this book!"

~ Linda Sullivan, Glendale, AZ

"Laurie is truly inspiring. Her chapters are amazing, and they always relate to me. I really love her insight on forgiving herself and how she did it. Not many people can forgive herself, even for minor mistakes. I hope that if I am ever in a place where I am lost and need to help myself forgive, Laurie and her book are the ones I will turn to."

~ Hailey, CO

"I just finished my 2nd read of the book. It was so nice I read it twice lol. But seriously, it's a great first book for someone wanting to dip their toes into some self-help awareness! It's not intimidating like a lot of the big reads out there. I've never finished a lot of the authors books that you quoted because they seemed overwhelming to me, so I love that you've read them and referenced them in your book and give examples for people to relate the advice with! I feel like this is a perfect 'self-love for dummies' book that any age, gender or any level of emotional maturity level adult could benefit from. I really hope you're planning to write another one! And you know my *struggle with boundaries so reading this gave me a big push to really set my intentions and expectations into action for this new year!"*

~ Whitney Nicole, Colorado Springs, CO

"This book is wonderfully packaged with enough information to jump start a turning point in anyone's life! I am blown away by the amount of courage it has taken for you to put this together. I've watched your whole journey in to becoming who you are today…. I lived many of these painful moments with you/ you have taken all that pain and turned it into something Amazing that you can share with so many others. I have personally learned so much from you while you've been 'learning' all these things. I have applied many of these principles in my life and never would have had the strength or knowledge without you."

~ Kimberly Nelson, Divide, CO

"Laurie has been amazing at teaching me how to become the best leader I can be, as well as just the best person I can be! She has helped me learn what teaching/learning styles suit me best, what type of leader I am, where I can grow and so much more! I cannot wait to see what she has in store for the future!"

~ Kat McDanial, Colorado Springs, CO

"Laurie Kroeger is very knowledgeable in what she does. She loves people and is always ready to help with a smile. I am so glad I got to meet Laurie and have gotten to know her better.

"Laurie is an outstanding coach! She really listens first, helps you to prioritize your schedule and leads by example. I would highly recommend giving Laurie a call to set up a coaching call."

~ Laura Odegard, Colorado Springs, CO

"Laurie is an excellent coach and thought leader. Very professional and connects with people very easily. She truly cares about your success. She is a great listener."

~ Charlotte Pierce, Puerto Rico

No part of this book may be reproduced in any form or by any electronic or mechanical means including information storage and retrieval systems, without permission in writing from the author.

This publication is designed to provide general information pertaining to the subject matter within. If legal advice or expert service is required, the services of a professional person should be retained.

ISBN: 979-8-9877309-0-4

Copyright © 2023 Laurie Kroeger

All Rights Reserved

DEDICATION & SPECIAL THANKS

This book is dedicated to the memory of June Rita Fern Pittman, my grandmother who is in heaven. Thank you, grandma, for having the heart of a Saint and teaching me to love. Family members often tell me how much I am just like Grandma June, with a big heart and love enough for everyone. I am proud to be that person. It has taken a long time for me to see it.

A special thank you to my parents. They all had one thing in common, faith. Faith that God would lead me where I needed to go. With the trials and tribulations, I created in my life, I thank God they continued to pray for me.

Thank you to my sister for always standing beside me. Thank you for the support, encouragement, and kick in the pants when I needed it most. You are and always have been my best friend.

And finally thank you to my husband who has supported me through the ups and downs and all my antics, not only while writing this book but over the past few years where, thanks to him, I have had the opportunity to learn and grow into the person I never knew I could be.

A note to my children and grandchildren, nieces and nephews: I love you all to the moon and back. You are my light and my inspiration to be better every day. I pray that you will discover the self-love and self-trust that will bring you all the happiness and success you want in life.

Contents

PREFACE

In this book my hope is that you will find the self-trust and self-love to lead you to the success you deserve. Be the leader of your life and love yourself as much as you love others with the love that has been inside of you this whole time.

I will share some of the messiest and most painful years, I call my "wonder years," and what it took to overcome them. We will walk through the beginning of my journey in taking back the power I had lost. As you read through these stories of mine and remember your own, you may feel emotions that were/are scary and uncomfortable, but necessary to take back your power. Emotions are the powerhouse to guide you to a happy and balanced life. How you handle your emotions will influence whether you react or respond to outside events and how your choices and behaviors will lead you back to the goals and desires you have left in the shadows. This is where you will start to find your peace, happiness, and sense of belonging. I will talk of belonging, authenticity, being your best self, and believing in the decisions and choices you make. I will cover what self-forgiveness is and how to leave your past in the rearview mirror. I will share the importance of whole-hearted leadership in your personal and professional life. And by the end of this book, you will discover that *loving you is easy.* I will recap the most important pieces of this book and leave you with tips, tools, and resources you can use to live your best life.

I wrote this book for you because you are worth it.

INTRODUCTION

What does it feel like when life seems to knock you down over and over? Does it make you want to do a happy dance every morning? Probably not. It's discouraging, frustrating, overwhelming and at times just plain irritating. It creates anger, anxiety, and depression. It's as if you are standing in a dump with garbage piled high and wide, in the pouring rain with no end in sight. Your mind decides to avoid the situation. So instead of working through the problems you stay out late drinking and partying, you eat every pint of ice cream, package of cookies and bag of chips you can find, or you dive deeper into work spending hours and hours working overtime to avoid the problems in your daily life. You start to use coping mechanisms, turning to forbidden fruits for comfort and a way to escape the undesirable outcomes. What you don't see, standing in that garbage dump, is just ahead, around the corner—the heights of joy, peace, happiness, and success. You just need to believe in your unlimited potential.

I say you, but this was me. I lived in that dump of a life for too long. I had to find a way out. I started by taking one step, then another, and another and before I realized it I was out of the dumps and on my way to my best life and striving to reach my greatest potential.

In the *15 Invaluable Laws of Growth*, by John Maxwell, "[t]he Law of Diminishing Intent says, 'The longer you wait to do something you should do now, the greater the odds that you will never actually do it.'"

Your first step was picking up this book. Don't stop here. You have unlimited potential that someone, somewhere has stifled or squashed. I don't care what bad decisions you have made; trust me you can make a difference in your life and the lives of those around you. I'm not saying this will be easy, and there may be people you leave behind. You are not leaving them because you are growing, you are leaving them because they are standing still and you are choosing to move forward.

You will find throughout the book how projecting love onto others was used as a tool for controlling, healing, or excusing poor behavior. At times it was my way of contributing or measuring my own self-worth. In the process of loving others, I forgot who I was, and believed I was not worthy of the same love I gave to others.

6

Loving you is easy, loving me is hard is based on my journey to get out of the mess I had created in my life. I was convinced that I would never amount to anything. A life of sex, drugs and.... I crawled my way out one step at a time. I have created a successful life because of my mistakes and in the process, I inadvertently discovered the meaning of peace, happiness, and gained a sense of belonging I didn't know was missing.

An unknown author offered this wisdom that I have found true through my journey: "it's not through healing that you will love yourself, it's through loving yourself that you will heal."

Does this mean I have it all together all the time? Nope, I am still a work in progress and so are you.

What you don't see, standing in that garbage dump, is just ahead, around the corner—the heights of joy, peace, happiness, and success. You just need to believe in your unlimited potential.

The stories you will read in this book are from my perspectives of my life. It doesn't mean my parents did anything wrong. They did the best they could with the information they had at the time.

I believe in God, and I give Him all the credit. You may not and that is ok, whether you believe in a higher power or the energies of the universe, what is important is to take what you need and leave the rest.

THE TRUTH BEHIND THE WOLF PACK

Many of us have seen the social media post with a large pack of wolves trekking through the snow. The caption talks about the leader leading from behind and ensuring no one gets left. This is a great story, but it is just that, a story. A story we can learn from and use as an analogy for leadership. (If you are interested in the full caption you can google, wolf pack leading from behind.)

The truth is, although wolves are natural caregivers, fun and intelligent, the weak and the sick are left behind, often to care for the young. Meanwhile the strongest is leading at the front, charging through the snow so the others can tread more easily.

Why is this truth important? In our society the strongest are seen as the leaders. The truth is we are all leaders, the strong, the perceived weak, the lost.

John Maxwell will tell you that "leadership is influence, nothing more, nothing less." As individuals we have influence on the people around us. Good or bad, we influence people every day. How we use that influence is what is important and determines our level of leadership.

When I was in my early 20's I was a shift leader for a large pizza chain. I had influence, what I said or did was essentially where the bar of expectation was set for the shift. Was I a good leader? I'd like to think so, but as a 20-year-old know it all I had some work to do. I didn't understand the value of communication, empathy or building strong relationships.

I lived an entire lifetime before I was legally able to drink. I was married at 16, had my daughter at 18 and was divorced by 20. How in the world could all of this have happened before I was 21? I asked myself that question many times. The answers didn't come until my early 40's, when I discovered I had been seeking a sense of belonging my entire life. Dozens of failed relationships, 4 marriages, 3 children and 4 grandchildren later I finally began to understand.

Wolves travel in family units. I had three family units. Wolves will follow the pack until they branch off to start their own families and lead their own pack. Some packs are stronger than others, each has its own leader, the parents, and the pack is only as strong as the leaders. I left my pack(s) to start my own pack, hoping I would find a sense of belonging I didn't know I had been longing for.

You may be thinking, how does this play into self-love, self-trust and what the hell does this have to do with me? That's a great question. Wolves must trust their instincts, believe in who they are and know each day is a new beginning with its own challenges that will have to be faced. Wolves do not dwell on the past as we often do, they do not mourn the loss of loved ones or allow external events to derail their goals for months, years or decades. They know that in order to survive and thrive they must keep moving forward.

As individuals we have influence on the people around us. Good or bad, we influence people every day. How we use that influence is what is important and determines our level of leadership.

CHAPTER ONE – THE FORBIDDEN FRUITS

I remember a time in my mid 20s when nothing seemed to go right. In the course of about 2 weeks, I managed to get two speeding tickets, the refrigerator in my apartment broke and my car needed a new starter. I was a broke mom! Seriously, what the heck world.

People would tell me, "What doesn't kill you, makes you stronger" or "Have faith, it'll work itself out." I wanted to scream! That was not helpful at all! However, I do believe in my heart that everything happens for a reason, even if we don't know what that reason is for years to come. It did work itself out and it did make me stronger and smarter.

I went to court for the tickets. One was dismissed and the other reduced to $180 and I was able to set up a payment plan. Lesson learned: Don't speed if you cannot afford the consequences. I have learned to slow down and plan for possible delays. Now, I tell my kids, and myself, "You can speed if you can afford the consequences." After a week with no refrigerator, I called the landlord and told him the refrigerator broke. He asked me why I waited so long to call him. He brought a new fridge the next day. Lesson learned: you must talk to people and ask for help to get things done. And finally, a friend helped me fix my car. Lesson learned: All things are possible with a little help and I learned how to change the starter in my car.

It all seemed overwhelming at the time as the "life" experiences piled on, but they did pass, and I did learn.

People by nature are good and have a desire to help those who want to make their lives better. It's ok to ask for help. Accept graciously when offered. However, if you are consistently seeking help and taking advantage of those who are offering, trust gets broken and the willingness for others to help will cease to exist.

Forbidden fruits, that which is desired strongly because it is not allowed, an indulgence or pleasure that is considered illegal, immoral or contradicts your values. Forbidden fruits are most often drugs, sex, alcohol, overeating, being a workaholic. It is anything used to numb or hide the pain, stuff emotions, and take away from living a happy peaceful life.

Why? Because you don't believe you deserve a happy, peaceful life. You don't believe there is an end in sight. You blame others for your unhappiness. When you make the initial decision to dive into the forbidden fruits, it is driven by emotions. Shame creates a desire to drown pain and suffering, forget bad memories, or an excuse to wallow in self-pity. Let's dive into self-pity, blame, and shame.

Self-Pity

Self-pity is an abundance of self-loathing, constant dwelling on the misfortunes in life and drowning in your sorrows and woes.

We like to have parties. We like to be around people and pity parties are no exception.

Sometimes you throw yourself a party and invite all of your greatest fears, insecurities, darkest emotions and debilitating self-limiting beliefs to attend as your guests of honor. This is a pity party, you are invited, no RSVP needed.

Self-pity is self-sabotage. What are you looking for when you decide to throw yourself a pity party? Why would you invite your friends or family?

I know now why I did. I was seeking validation for my feelings, I was seeking to remove the loneliness I felt inside and somehow I believed if I dwelled on it long enough and complained loud enough someone else would solve the problems for me. Trust me when I say it doesn't work that way.

Have you ever noticed friends and family starting to distance themselves? Do you get angry because your friends cancel plans with you and decide to go fishing instead?

This happens unconsciously or even intentionally, to avoid the self-deprecating conversations you are engaging in, the constant whining about why life is so hard, and the excuses and justifications you use as to why you cannot make changes in your life.

They love you and don't enjoy watching you beat yourself up on a daily basis. They have offered advice and solutions you don't apply, they've provided you with options you've dismissed, ultimately saying to them I choose to live in the misery that is my life. The distance between you and your loved ones completely derails your goal of removing loneliness and having your feelings validated. You begin to feel lonelier, shameful, and start to blame them for not being there when you needed them most. And the cycle feeding into the forbidden fruits continues.

I had a friend, every time we were together, I was consistently reassuring her that she was a good person. She had a great job, amazing kids, she was funny and crazy intelligent. However, given the option to spend time with her or go do something else, I would often choose to do something else, even if it was laundry. It was exhausting being around someone I constantly had to lift up. When she was given opportunities to grow or change, she would make excuses about why she couldn't. If I did spend time with her, I could only handle an hour or so before I needed to rest. The constant negativity was mentally and emotionally draining.

Another one, a guy I was dating, would point out the flaws in others. He was generally a nice person. However, when we were out, he would criticize people. He would criticize their looks, the way they walked, or the shoes they had on their feet. I would think to myself, *Does he say these things about me when I am not around?* His negativity created doubt and broken trust.

I have learned that when we criticize or judge others that is where we often judge ourselves the harshest. I knew this was someone I did not want to be around for the rest of my life.

How do you get out of a pity party?

What would you tell a friend? Would you say, *We're in this together, you can do this, I'm here for you, I've got your back?* You are always willing to do so much for others, but it seems too much to do for yourself. Why is that? Somewhere you learned to believe that you are not enough.

Listen to me now. You are enough, you are just as perfect as any other human being in this world. Trust me, this one took a minute for me to accept. Every person in this world has their demons. No one escapes the world of emotions and everyone makes mistakes. But you can learn to acknowledge them and move forward.

Start by acknowledging the feelings you are experiencing. What you are feeling is normal. You are meant to feel. You are human.

Take responsibility for your actions and your thoughts. Behind every negative thought about who you are is a lie you have been told and have chosen to believe.

Be kind and compassionate to yourself, you are your own best friend. You have the capacity for amazing love. You use it regularly with others. That same, amazing love for others, that is inside of you, is there for you too. You cannot love others more than you love yourself.

Show yourself empathy. Feel your feelings, what are they telling you? Take action! You are the hero in your story. Own it, believe it, live it!

Wake Forest University defined "[e]motions [as] real-time data sparked by sensations in the body. Feelings can be more biased, altered by mental misconceptions."

Feelings and emotions tell you it's time to make a change. You feel hungry, it's time to eat. You feel hurt, it's time to reflect. Did you stub your toe or did your best friend lie to you? Anger, discontent and sadness are emotions that can be brought on by hunger, physical pain or feeling hurt. When you allow yourself to feel the hurt and sadness you can then choose to move out of those feelings, but you cannot ignore them. You cannot pretend to be ok.

When you ignore your feelings you bottle up what you are feeling inside. The feelings don't just go away, and eventually the cap on that bottle gives and an explosion of uncontrollable emotions drive actions you normally wouldn't engage in.

Anger is often the first to rear its ugly head. You start to raise your voice, say things you didn't mean, or worse, you get physically violent taking out all of your pent-up feelings on objects or those closest to you.

Depression is another one that shows up when you stuff your emotions. You have too much weighing on your mind and believe you will never get out, the sadness overtakes you and you just want to curl up and lay in bed all day. Regret creeps in, shame builds and the blame game starts again. You turn to your preferred forbidden fruits.

I am unsure who stated this originally, but "[s]ometimes life doesn't go your way, and you can feel frustrated, angry, and upset. Everyone experiences this, and it's up to you to choose how you'll react to difficult times. It may be

No one escapes the world of emotions, and everyone makes mistakes. But you can learn to acknowledge them and move forward into better days.

tempting to feel negative but using positive phrases and words can make a huge difference. In reality, life will always have ups and downs, and true happiness isn't a life without problems. True happiness is the ability to deal with whatever comes your way, even if you find yourself in an unpleasant situation."

Blame

Forbidden fruits lie and you believe it's not your fault. You begin to play the blame game. Blame is the belief that others are responsible for your pain and suffering. You blame other people for your actions and behaviors. Have you ever said, *she made me do it?* or *I didn't really want to but I had to.* Taking responsibility for your decisions means making hard choices. She really didn't make you, you chose to, for some unknown reason.

Perhaps it was to show you were strong, or brave or loyal. Whatever the reason you still made a choice.

Often, we blame an event in our lives for the way we live. We blame the circumstances of our situation for not reaching our goals and we fail to see how our choices keep us where we are.

Perhaps you were in a car accident that kept you out of work for an extended period of time and you lost your job. That sucks, no doubt and I am sorry if that happened to you.

Now you have recovered. You are broke, you're about to lose your house, and your spouse is on the verge of leaving. You blame the accident or the idiot driving for your misfortune. You throw regular pity parties and invite the most important guests of honor, those fears, darkest emotions, the debilitating self-limiting beliefs and your greatest insecurities. You make a choice to stay in your pity party, you choose not to move forward and find other options. You choose to ignore your spouse when he/she says, "Let's try something different."

There are events that happen in life that will change your path and the direction you thought you were headed. The key is to accept the changes, pivot, move out of your comfort zone, leave the pity party behind and take control. Become the person who can and will make a difference because of the circumstances instead of letting the circumstances control your life.

We have all blamed others for our misfortunes at some point in our lives. It is human nature. We regret decisions we made or actions we have taken.

How are you going to handle the next situation that comes into your life?

To remove the blame game from your life, take responsibility for your actions and decisions. Shit happens, stuff occurs and life goes on. Sometimes you feel that you didn't do anything to deserve the hand you were dealt and that could very well be a true statement. However, you are responsible for how you choose to react or respond in any given situation.

Talk about your mistakes and take ownership of your choices. Be vulnerable; vulnerability is strength. Having the courage to admit a mistake or wrongdoing and accept the consequences of your choices will help you to grow in your integrity.

22

Integrity builds character, character builds confidence.

I love Brené Brown's definition of integrity and I work

The key is to accept the changes, pivot, move out of your comfort zone, leave the pity party behind and take control.

to live by it daily: "Integrity is choosing courage over comfort; choosing what is right over what is fun, fast, or easy; and choosing to practice our values rather than simply professing them."

Shame

I was living in Colorado after my first divorce. Living in one place, then another and yet another. I sent my daughter, almost 3 years old, to live with her dad, 1300 miles away. Her dad was an amazing man, he was kind, intelligent, handsome, thoughtful (most of the time) and he was funny. He was one of the most laid-back people I have ever met, nothing seemed to faze him. The only reason we divorced was because I was homesick and ran away. When he flew in to pick her up, he was planning to ask me to come home with him but for whatever reason, he didn't. If he had I would have said yes. But then I wouldn't be where I am today. Everything happens for a reason.

I was ashamed of my decision to leave with our daughter without talking to him. Sending her away was one of the hardest moments in my life and it was the catalyst to the downward spiral into what my sister likes to call, the wonder years. Those years when you wonder, what the hell was I thinking and how did I live through it?

I was full of shame, I could not provide a good stable home for my daughter. I was alone. I blamed everyone else because, at the age of 20, I had no idea what the hell I was doing, no job, no daycare, no place to live and no help. I regretted that I could not give this beautiful little girl the life she deserved.

Before she was even born I had big dreams about the amazing life she would have. I had it all planned out, dance schools, gymnastics, family vacations, college and so much more. It was my dream of the perfect family life. Tears stream down my face as I recall those days. She was (is) my world, I loved her more than life itself.

After I sent her to live with her dad, I tried to move forward, but the pain and shame were weighing on me heavily. I was in a dark place even when the sun was shining bright.

> *I was full of shame…and I blamed everyone else…*

Forbidden fruits feed shame. Shame is defined as a painful feeling of humiliation or distress caused by the consciousness of wrong or foolish behavior. Brené Brown, a researcher at the University of Houston, defines it as an "intensely painful feeling or experience of believing that we are flawed and therefore unworthy of love." The difference between shame and guilt: shame says, *I am a bad person* and guilt says, *I did something bad*. Brown continued with, "[w]e desperately don't want to experience shame, and we're not willing to talk about it. Yet the only way to resolve shame is to talk about it. Maybe we're afraid of topics like love and shame. Most of us like safety, certainty, and clarity. Shame and love are grounded in vulnerability and tenderness."

One night, alone in the basement of my parents' home, I held the biggest pity party of my life. I invited all of the guests of honor, all of my greatest fears; judgement, rejection, criticism. My insecurities; *I'm not pretty; I'm not smart; Nobody likes me; Everybody hates me; Think I'll go eat worms.* I invited even my darkest emotions; regret, sadness, despair, anger, and my most debilitating self-limiting beliefs; *I'm worthless; I will never be good enough; I am nobody!*

I decided to end it, all of it; the pain, the hurt, and the disgust in myself. This world would be better off without me in it. I was tired and I just wanted to sleep forever.

Thankfully a decision <u>without</u> action is just that, a decision. I was terrified of death. *What would happen to my beautiful daughter? What would my parents and my sisters and brothers think? Would they blame themselves?*

Even though I hated myself, I loved them so much, I couldn't do it.

Steve Maraboli, a decorated military veteran and philanthropist, said, in his book *Unapologetically You: Reflections on Life and the Human Experience*, "[w]e all make mistakes, have struggles, and even regret things in our past. But you are not your mistakes, you are not your struggles, and you are here NOW with the power to shape your day and your future."

More shame, blame and regret. But with that came a new determination to become better. And another utter failure. FAIL = First Attempt In Learning. I still didn't like who I was, I had no real friends, I believed my family hated me because of the decisions I was making, and I had nowhere to turn for support.

This was one of the scariest times in my life. The decisions I was making only made matters worse. I felt like I could do nothing right.

After I had my second child, I started hanging out with people who used meth (my forbidden fruit), these became my people, as long as I had money to buy from them. I belonged. I fit in. "Friends" would come to visit as long as I had a supply, I was less alone. I would buy more, and share, even though I couldn't afford it. I need to show that I loved them. I needed them to feel they were important to me so I would feel important to them and on occasion they would even share with me.

Meanwhile, I was destroying my life. I did all the things I thought I needed to so I could *fit in* and *belong* regardless of the people or environment I was in. I felt accepted.

I learned at an early age how to fit in. I was raised with 3 sets of parents. My family tree looks like a monster grove of aspens. Have you ever seen the root system of an aspen grove?

Let me clarify this one for you. There is my mom and her husband, my biological dad and his wife, and my adopted dad and his wife (he adopted me when he married my mom and they had my sister.) Each with their own rules, values and beliefs.

I was raised mostly as an only child and lived primarily with my mother. We moved around; 4 schools by the fourth grade. I spent most of my adolescent and tween years bouncing between my mom and my adopted dad, where I would have time with my younger sister and brother. I would get to visit my biological dad and my older brother every few years, until I went to live with them in Alaska at age 14.

I discovered in my journey for self-acceptance, that this is where I learned to be who I thought they needed me to be in each distinct family unit. I could change at the drop of a hat to meet the needs of any situation.

Losing yourself to the acceptance of others will ultimately cause you to lose acceptance of yourself. You feel inadequate and distorted perfection seems the only way to prove your

worth. Distorted perfection is learning how to perfect behaviors in any situation, good or bad.

With my "friends," I learned how to inspect what I was buying to make sure I was getting "good" quality, I learned how to use a scale, easiest math lesson ever, I learned to speak the language and how to communicate with other users, I learned when to keep my mouth shut and stay in the background. Eventually, I failed and I was not able to maintain the facade.

> *Distorted perfection is learning how to perfect behaviors in any situation, good or bad.*

When you fail and are unable to achieve this so-called perfection; shame, blame, and regret drive you deeper into despair.

Regret is a feeling you get that tells you that you have made a mistake, a poor choice of words, or an action that hurt yourself or someone else unintentionally. When you do or say something that feeds regret, you feel shame.

Shame is not all bad if it is focused towards a behavior, it can help you to see areas where you can grow. However, when shame is used as a personal attack it can derail your entire life. During the covid pandemic, shame was used as a tactic as an attempt to force people comply with the directives.

You should be ashamed of yourself! You are a horrible person! I can't believe you would.... Perhaps you have heard these words. They are personal attacks on you as a person and said often enough can cause you to believe them and you make choices to confirm it.

You should be ashamed of your behavior. This says in essence, *I don't like what you did.* This leaves room for growth and it is a choice. It says here is an opportunity to learn from a mistake and make it right. The former attacks on yourself can leave you feeling worthless and not enough.

According to an article in Scientific American, June Tangney of George Mason University has studied shame for decades. In numerous collaborations with Ronda L. Dearing of the University of Houston and others, she has found that people who have a propensity for feeling shame—a trait termed shame-proneness—often have low self-esteem (which means, conversely, that a certain degree of self-esteem may protect us from excessive feelings of shame)" "Tangney and her co-authors explained it well in a 2005 paper: "A shame-prone individual who is reprimanded for being late to work after a night of heavy drinking might be likely to think, 'I'm such a loser; I just can't get it together,' whereas a guilt-prone individual would more likely think, 'I feel badly for showing up late. I inconvenienced my coworkers.' Feelings of shame can be painful and debilitating, affecting one's core sense of self, and may invoke a self-defeating cycle of negative affect.... In comparison, feelings of guilt, though painful, are less disabling than shame and are likely to motivate the individual in a positive direction toward reparation or change."

How do we overcome shame? SHINE A LIGHT ON IT!

Talk about it with someone you trust. Shining a light on it does not mean airing your dirty laundry to the world. Start with a counselor, therapist, or your pastor. It's important to talk with someone you trust, who has your best interests at heart, who will not judge and can extend empathy and compassion as you share. The who, what, when and where are important to remember. Otherwise, you will end up right back in your shame storm and trying to back track by blaming others.

Brené Brown said that "[i]f you put shame in a petri dish and cover it with judgment, silence, and secrecy, you've created the perfect environment for shame to grow until it makes its way into every corner and crevice of your life. If, on the other hand, you put shame in a petri dish and douse it with empathy, shame loses its power and begins to wither. Empathy creates a hostile environment for shame—an environment it can't survive in, because shame needs you to believe you're alone and it's just you."

Sometimes you do or say things that you feel bad about. Talk about it. Bring it to the surface and admit where you went wrong. I am sure you have heard actions speak louder than words. You can apologize over and

Feeding our feelings of regret, feed into shame, and leaves us feeling worthless and not enough.

over, but if you don't change your behavior people will not trust your apologies, regardless of how sincere you may be. It takes time and follow through to rebuild trust that has been broken. Bringing your mistakes into the light will remove the power of shame and give you an opportunity to make things right. We will talk more about building trust in a later chapter.

CHAPTER TWO – THE STORIES BEHIND THE SCENES

It's hard to discern the stories you tell yourself from the truth. The stories are so ingrained in your everyday thinking that they feel as if they are a part of who you are. The stories are just emphasized parts of the truth.

The lyrics from Francesca Battistelli' song "Behind the Scenes" captures this part-of-a-truth idea: "Things aren't always what they seem. You're only seeing part of me. There's more than you could ever know behind the scenes,"

Have you ever had a chance to look behind the curtains at a popular play or Broadway show? What you see, as a part of the audience, is the magic that happens on stage, the lights, the actors and the scenes that have been created to show you what they want you to see. What you don't see are all the blunders, the problems and the failures that result in you having the best experience.

Every actor, producer, engineer, costume artist and director has doubts and fears. Every scene has been recreated over and over. The lighting, costumes and scenes are all trial and error. It takes someone who is willing to look beyond the problems. Someone who knows you have to fail to succeed. Someone who can decipher the facts and generate a solution to every situation they encounter. This is how the magic happens.

Life is similar. The stories you tell yourself are problems and every problem has a solution. Taking time to analyze the facts and uncover the self-limiting beliefs gives you the ability to generate solutions for any problem you will face.

My favorite stories go something like this: *I don't have what I need, and I have no idea where to find it. This is just too hard, and I don't have the resources I need to accomplish my goal.* I use this one often. It has stopped me in my tracks more than once. Another one I use is: *I don't know what I am doing wrong. I keep trying and trying, failing and failing, trying and trying some more. I just can't seem to get it right.* **What is wrong with me?**

You can overcome these and similar thoughts to recreate the scenes in your life, you can adjust the lighting to shine where it highlights the best parts of you. You can look beyond the problem and generate a solution to every situation. You are enough!

There are many stories you tell yourself; most are not true. Some of the stories you believe have been handed down from generation to generation. You tell yourself, *I can't do something because it's not in my blood* or *this is just who I am*. Often, you believe what other people think or perceive about you and it creates fear and anxiety. You believe that you can't be successful because someone, somewhere said you couldn't.

One story I heard often, "you will never amount to anything," usually preceded with "if you continue this behavior." But all I heard was "you will never amount to anything" and I believed what was being said, I would give up on things before they even had a chance to succeed.

Other stories often used to justify why you cannot accomplish your goals are: *The time is not right; I am too old or too young; I don't have the skills or education;* or *I have too many other responsibilities*. These are the stories that derail where you want to be.

I have also recognized many of these stories throughout my life. *I cannot take care of my children because I am never going to amount to anything. I can love you, but I am not worthy of love because I have made too many bad decisions. I will never have a great career because I didn't go to college. I cannot go to college because I have no time, no money and I have to work to take care of my children. I'll do it when....* All these stories slowed down the progress I could have made. However, everything happens for a reason.

I moved to Wisconsin to work as a nanny for my oldest brother who had been adopted. My mother was only 17 when she had him. I learned about him when I was in my 20's. By the grace of God, he was brought into our lives. My 3rd child was about 2 months old, I had lost custody of my 2nd, and as you know, I gave up custody of my 1st. My brother's wife was pregnant with their first. They needed a nanny. I said yes, I needed a change, something different. As it turns out, it will be one of the best decisions I have ever made. It changed the course of my life.

As I have mentioned a few times, I believe with every fiber of my being that everything happens for a reason. God uses our mistakes.

I was living in the living room of my mom's one bedroom house with her husband, too many cats and my newborn son. I really felt that I will never amount to anything. I had no idea how I was going to survive. When the opportunity came to take a leap of faith, I took it. Sometimes a big change is the best way to get out of a less than ideal situation.

My brother and sister-in-law had 3 rules when I agreed to move in with them: go to church, no smoking and go back to school to get my degree. The first two were relatively easy, it was February in Wisconsin and colder than the heart of Cruella Deville. Since I couldn't smoke in the house and I had no desire to stand outside, I was able to quit, at least for a while. Church was a part of my childhood so it wasn't much of a stretch. However, going back to school to get my degree, that was a challenge. I had already taken several courses at a community college. I did well, but I still didn't believe I could actually succeed in college. Remember, I would never amount to anything. I wasn't smart enough and I had no idea what I wanted to be when I grew up.

Kirk Douglas once said in his book *The Ragman's Son*, "[t]he biggest lie is the lie we tell ourselves in the distorted visions we have of ourselves, blocking out some sections, enhancing others. What remains are not the cold facts of life, but how we perceive them. That's really who we are."

School didn't start until the next fall. I made up as many excuses I could find as to why I couldn't start classes. Stories such as: they haven't posted the fall calendar, or I was too late to sign up for the classes I needed, or the prerequisite class I need, for this one course, is full.

Stories lie. The story will try to tell you that you will fail, you are worthless, you cannot accomplish what you want, you can't trust your decisions and many more.

Procrastination was my go-to excuse for most things. But with every excuse there was a solution. Finally, with a little pushing and encouragement from my brother and sister-in-law, I did it. I enrolled in college part time at the age of 26. It took 4 years to complete my associates degree, but I did it. One step at a time. And it felt great. A real accomplishment. I started to believe in myself, just a little. I could amount to something, if I would just do it. I started to see that maybe, just maybe I could be a better person. I could learn to make better decisions. Rewrite my story.

Don't let the lies stop you from growing. Take that leap of faith. I know you can do it!

Because, when, but and if — the most powerful words you can use to destroy your life.

I'll start writing when I have more time, or when inspiration hits just right. I'll start working on that project but I just have too many other things on my plate right now. I can't do this because no one really cares. I am not ready for this because I have to work full time. I'm not good enough because I don't have multiple degrees. No one will love me because I am too much or not enough. It's too hard because I just don't know where to start. I should be perfect because everyone else is. I would if time allowed. I might be able to if I could just wrap my head around it. If only I could sit still for a while, I would be able to solve the problem. I would but, I should but, I can but, maybe when, when this is done, when the kids are grown, when life gets <u>easier</u>.

"The most difficult part of our stories is often what we bring to them—what we make up about who we are and how we are perceived by others. Yes, maybe we lost our job or screwed up a project, but what makes that story so painful is what we tell ourselves about our own self-worth and value," said Brené Brown.

Among many others these are the statements that started the stories I would, and at times still, tell myself. They are always preceded or followed by the justifications *because, when, if,* or *but.* You often justify your actions or lack thereof with a story, an excuse. Listen to the excuses you tell yourself and you will uncover your limiting beliefs.

I would venture to say 99% of the stories you tell yourself have little or no truth behind them. When you stop and look at the facts involved, you will find it was your choices, decisions and actions or lack of action that led you into the positions you find yourself in.

The stories you use to guide you most often are self-sabotaging. What is self-sabotage?

According to an article *What Is Self-Sabotage? How to Help Stop the Vicious Cycle* by Christina R. Wilson, Ph.D, "[s]elf-sabotage occurs when we destroy ourselves physically, mentally, or emotionally or deliberately hinder our own success and wellbeing by undermining personal goals and values.

"Self-sabotage, also known as behavioral dysregulation, can be conscious or unconscious depending on level of awareness. An example of conscious self-sabotage is deciding to eat cake, despite a goal to eat healthy. Unconscious self-sabotage happens when a personal goal or value has been undermined but not initially recognized.

"Someone with a fear of failure might wait until the last minute to work on an important project, unconsciously avoiding the prospect of advancement.

"Another dimension of self-sabotage is cognitive dissonance. Cognitive dissonance is the internal imbalance or discomfort experienced when words or actions do not align with beliefs and values. When this happens, we act to ease the discomfort by changing our words or behaviors or by reframing our goals and values."

We will get into values in Chapter 5. Here is what I know, without goals and values you will base your decision on feelings and emotions. Learning how to base your decisions on what is important to you will change the way you think about what you can achieve.

A mistake is just a decision where you didn't like the outcome.

Speaking on decisions, "[i]n any moment of decision, the best thing you can do is the right thing, the next best thing is the wrong thing, and the worst thing you can do is nothing." This statement is often attributed to Theodore Roosevelt.

How to start rewriting your story:

1. **Write down or reflect on the story**. What is the story/excuse you have been telling yourself that is preventing you from reaching or even setting your goals, what emotions and self-limiting beliefs are driving that story? Is it fear? Are you afraid people will laugh at you for trying? Are you afraid you will fail? Are you afraid you may actually succeed?

   This was a big one for me. I was afraid of who I would become if I were successful. I used to believe successful people were selfish, lifted high on their horse and better than everyone else. This story limited my ability to accomplish what I wanted. I did not want to become that type of person and would self-sabotage my own progress. And then, I met two of the most amazing successful people in my life—Robert and Venessa Raymond! They showed me that successful people do have a heart, they believed in me, more than I believed in myself. Their encouragement, faith in me and love instilled in me the desire to achieve what I never thought I could.

2. **What are the facts about the event that occurred?** "Just the facts ma'am," said Jack Webb in Dragnet. When you look at the event that took place, you can see it more objectively. A car hit me, I was in the hospital, I was unable to work. My friend lied about something, what was the motivation for the lie? Were they afraid I would explode or unfriend them on Facebook? Now what?

By looking at the actual event you are better equipped to generate a solid solution. You can approach your friend and communicate using empathy, compassion, and knowledge. You can move past the accident that landed you in the hospital and create a goal that will help you become the person you want to be.

3. **Reflect or write down the choices you made**. When I was living in the wonder years, I was driven by emotions and trying to look at the facts was a real challenge. Fact: I made the decision to leave Alabama with my daughter when she was 2. I did not prepare for a big move and made an emotional, spur of the moment decision. I made the decision to send her back to live with her dad. I did what I believed was best for her and me at the time.

4. **Take responsibility for your choices and actions**. I had to admit I was not prepared to provide a quality life for my daughter. You will see later in this book I made many more poor choices that led me into a rabbit hole I never thought I would escape from.

    When you take responsibility for choices, actions and decisions you stop playing the blame game. Remember, when you point your finger at someone else there are three more pointing back at you. Instead of saying *you did this to me,* change it to *this happened and now I can choose what to do next*. Everything you need is inside of you. The information is available and accessible. You get to decide how to move forward.

5. **Rewrite the story avoiding the emotions that come with the event**. When rewriting the story, it's important to understand you are the hero. Even if you've made bad decisions, you made it through and you are here NOW, learning how to move forward. When I gave up custody of my daughter, I did it for her benefit. I made a decision with the information I had available to me at the time. A mistake is just a decision where you didn't like the outcome.

Mistakes happen, everyone makes them. It is a part of life. How you choose to react or respond to those mistakes will determine how your life will progress. An old man once said, "Erasers are made for those who make mistakes." A youth replied, "Erasers are made for those willing to correct their mistakes."

The stories you tell yourself cloud your judgment and self-awareness. Self-awareness is the ability to be aware of your reactions, emotions and decisions. To see yourself clearly and objectively. This can be hard depending on how you were raised and the belief systems you have ingrained into your mind. Self-awareness theory is based on the idea that you are not your thoughts, but the entity observing your thoughts; you are the thinker, separate and apart from your thoughts (Duval & Wicklund, 1972).

Mistakes happen, everyone makes them. It is a part of life. How you choose to react or respond to those mistakes will determine how your life will progress.

Having a good level of self-awareness gives you the ability to discern fact from feeling. I learned about self-awareness when I was working in corporate America. I started with a book called Emotional Intelligence 2.0. One of the most impactful messages I learned from this book was to stop treating my feelings as good or bad.

Feelings are a moment in time that give you an opportunity to make a decision or a change. TalentSmart is a great resource for beginning the process of understanding and growing in your own self-awareness. We will go more in depth later, but self-awareness is a major factor in overcoming the stories and the self-limiting beliefs that have derailed your progress.

Consider what Carl Gustav Jung said that "[e]verything that irritates us about others can lead us to an understanding of ourselves."

CHAPTER THREE – THE WONDER YEARS: A JOURNEY INTO ACCEPTANCE

For this chapter we are going to take a step back in time to the wonder years. Those are the early 20's, in my case, when I wondered, what the hell was I thinking and how in God's name did I live through it! I will show you how the forbidden fruits and the stories behind the scenes led me down a dark path that should have taken my life more than once and how I was able to get through them.

Often in your lives you find many different coping mechanisms. Chances are you didn't choose the healthy ones right off the bat. Everyone goes through something difficult in their lives. Loss of family, abuse, divorce, codependency, even those who seem to have grown up in the "perfect" home have their challenges. No one escapes the challenges in life. No one.

Different events in your life leave you in emotional turmoil. Fear, anger, confusion, worry, doubt and anxiety are the most common emotions that derail your ability to reason. These emotions pave the way for your brain to create the stories that lead to your self-limiting beliefs in life. How you choose to deal with these emotions determines your level of success or failure in relationships, work, and family.

Believe it or not, my mom will tell you I was an easy child. I didn't get angry. I didn't fight. I didn't always do what I was told, but I was not a difficult child. My mom recalls a time in the 3rd or 4th grade when the school had a program on dealing with anger. I came home after attending this class and started punching my pillow. She asked "What's wrong? Why are you punching your pillow?" I told her about the class and that I was supposed to punch a pillow when I was angry. She asked me, "What are you angry about?" I said, "I'm not, I'm just practicing."

Life was good, until it wasn't. Let's start with a little history.

I don't recall all the details or circumstances, but I seem to remember asking my mom if I could go live with my biological dad when I was 14 years old. She said yes. So, in June, I went to Alaska to live with my father. Alaska held yet another new set of rules, values, expectations and challenges.

It took a while to adjust. I remember sitting in the basement for hours and hours playing Mario Bros. I spent so many hours playing this game that I started to dream I was Mario and I would bang my head on the headboard trying to hit all the "?" blocks.

I was shy and it was hard making friends, especially since my last several attempts were a little less than successful. Once school started, I was able to make a few acquaintances and even what I would say was one real friend.

This one still stands out in my mind. I loved her, she was my best friend. Only the second best friend I had ever had, not including my sister. There was something about her. We could talk for hours. I remember one day we went horseback riding in the woods. There was a thin layer of snow on the ground. I was nervous as we crossed a small creek rippling under a wooden bridge. The bridge was icy and I had only been on a horse once or twice before. She talked me through it, gave me the confidence to calm the horse, get over the bridge and we had the most incredible ride.

Sometimes you need a friend who can help you get over the bridge. Someone who will believe in you until you believe in yourself.

I like to believe we connected, I felt she was like me. She had the ability to be what others needed her to be at any given moment. We had a rare, authentic connection. Finally, I felt I had someone I could relate to and really get to know. We would spend time together after school and "hang-out" like the "normal" kids did. I felt like I belonged. And then she was gone.

In May of the following year, my family had to move. We packed up, left Alaska and moved to Alabama. The reasons behind the move are not my story to tell but know it was a difficult and challenging time for the whole family. Between the 7th and 10th grade there were 4 more schools. Always the new kid. Before the end of the 10th grade, I ran away from home, quit school and got married.

Sometimes you need a friend who can help you get over the bridge. Someone who will believe in you until you believe in yourself.

The story that I told myself through most of my school years was, "it's not worth trying to make friends, if I keep them at arm's length I won't get hurt when they are gone." I built a wall around my heart. I would give anything to help others. I would do just about anything to make others happy and get to know them. However, I did not give them an opportunity to get to know me. It was too hard when it was time to move on. If they didn't get close to me, neither of us would be hurt when we went our separate ways. I chose to distance myself.

I later learned this perspective described by Jodi Picoult, in *My Sisters Keeper*, "[l]et me tell you this: if you meet a loner, no matter what they tell you, it's not because they enjoy solitude. It's because they have tried to blend into the world before, and people continue to disappoint them."

Fast forward a few years. Divorced, alone in Colorado, lost, and still trying to be what everyone else needed me to be. I was still avoiding intimate connections and relationships. I created a facade that covered the real pain behind who I thought I was, and that was nothing, at least, nothing important to anyone.

There are many jumbled memories from this period of my life. I dated a warlock, a demon, a sinner, or five, and one saint. As we talk about coping mechanisms, and I struggle to put together a timeline for the wonder years, I think to myself, give me a cigarette now or I will be drunk by noon, it's 11:56. We will talk about emotions being the driving force in a later chapter. But this chapter has been an emotional rollercoaster and a learning experience for me as I uncover more and more of those self-limiting beliefs and the lies I told myself.

I discovered with my body I could show "love" and make men happy and gain acceptance and belonging. Sex (love), Drugs (friends), more sex more drugs, rinse and repeat for about 4 years.

Somewhere in this time frame I started working for the pizza place. There, I met a saint who I would spend the next 4+ years with on and off. This man would have given me the moon, the stars and the sun if I had asked. He put up with more from me than any other person in my life at that time. I really wanted to marry him but I never felt I was enough. He even helped my sister and her family, long after I was gone. And still does almost 25 years later.

In my mind, as I would come and go, in and out of this and other relationships, I believed that I was doing them a favor.

In the middle of the wonder years and about two years into the on and off with my saint, I started dating a man 25 years older than me. He had long hair, played the bass guitar and seemed to be a fun guy. Days would go by and I wouldn't hear from him. He would call in sick for work and I worried about him. I would go to his place and bang on his door for what seemed like hours. I remember one afternoon I banged on the door for over an hour, knowing he was in the apartment, needing to see him just to make sure he was alive. Eventually, he stumbled to the door, still drunk from the night before.

I believed I could fix him. I thought, *if I could show him someone cared about him, he would have a reason to stop drinking*. I thought, *I can love this pain out of him*. Actually, I believed this in several of my relationships.

After a few months with him, I found I was pregnant and still making really bad choices. I knew that I didn't want to continue worrying about whether he would be around or drunk or worse. I told him, "I don't expect anything from you," and left. Shortly after my son was born, I remarried.

Story time:

> I was not the person they wanted to be with.
> I was not good enough for them.
> I cannot have a solid, stable relationship.
> I am unlovable.
> I must leave before they do.
> I don't deserve this, I gotta go!
> I am nobody.
> more "love," more "friends"

Marriage #2. Not much to say about this one, he was a really nice guy, caring, intelligent and funny, but he was not prepared for the baggage I carried around with me. Once again, I left. I still believed I was not enough. We were divorced in less than 18 months.

I moved back in with my saint and we spent another year or so together. After a short time, I moved into the apartment just below him. Close enough that I knew he was there, but I needed some separation. I felt vulnerable. I actually loved him. I needed to get away before he got too close. Of course, I didn't know that's what I was doing until much later in life.

I believe this is when I really started hanging out with "friends." More "friends" and another "love."

Marriage #3. We will call him Charlie, for safety's sake. I met Charlie through some friends at work. He was tall, handsome and had the most amazing blue eyes I had ever seen. He was a "bad boy" with tattoos and everything. He was the complete opposite of my saint. In the beginning, he was strong and attentive. After just a few short weeks, he wanted to get married, he said he never wanted to lose me. I thought, *Wow, he really loves me*! So, we did. We went to the courthouse and 15 minutes and two signatures later it was done and my life would never be the same.

It only took a few short weeks after the I-dos the honeymoon phase wore off. I started to learn that Charlie was controlling and abusive. I had no idea what I had gotten myself into. "Bad boy" didn't even come close. One night my son, almost 4 years old, was behaving strangely. Super agitated, biting on his cheek and his lips. It was in the wee hours of the morning and he bit a hole through his lip, it was bleeding profusely. I rushed him to the ER. I had no idea what was going on.

The hospital said he had ingested meth and someone had tried to counteract it with a downer. I don't remember this, but I have been told that I removed my child from the hospital and took him home, as instructed by Charlie. I was confused, distraught and terrified. I didn't understand. I loved this little boy. The last thing I ever wanted was for him to be hurt or affected by my poor choices. But he was, in a major way. I would have done anything for him, if I had only known what to do.

Ultimately, I lost custody of my son and he was placed in a temporary foster home. I did everything the courts said, lie detector tests to prove I did not give him the drugs, drug tests to prove I was trying, and supervised visits. Charlie refused all of them. When I moved out of my apartment, I found paraphernalia tucked between my son's mattress and box spring. I have reason to believe Charlie drugged my son intentionally, but I could never prove it.

One night, I arrived home after a supervised visit with my son. Charlie had cut the phone cord before I got there. This was back in the day when most phones were still attached to walls. Cell phones were just becoming popular. He accused me of cheating on him and tried to smother me with a pillow on my couch. I couldn't breathe, I was thrashing and kicking, and absolutely terrified. No matter how much I begged and pleaded, swore up and down that I did not cheat on him, he wouldn't stop. Somehow, I found the strength to push off all 6'4, 275 lbs of him. I managed to get away, crawled to the door and ran to my neighbors. I stayed at a friend's house for a while. I filed a domestic violence report, but nothing happened.

Charlie called one day and said he was getting ready to leave town and wanted to talk to me. For whatever reason, I agreed. We sat in my car and talked. He was telling me how much he loved me and wanted me in his life. He asked if I would leave town with him. When I said no, he grabbed me around my neck in a choke hold and started beating on me like a punching bag. I couldn't move, but I managed to get my knee on the horn and held it there for what seemed like an eternity as he pummeled my face. Eventually he jumped out of the car and ran off. I put my car in gear and drove like a bat out of hell and went to the hospital. At the hospital,

I discovered he had fractured my skull just above my right eye. I filed charges, a permanent restraining order and he went to prison for two years. "Crime of passion" they said, even though he tried to kill me, twice. My son's father eventually got custody and I left my son, thinking he's better off without me.

About 6 months later I started dating another guy. More "love." I stayed in this relationship for a short while and became pregnant with baby #3. The boyfriend was dealing at the time, and I was still hanging with "friends." Depression was my only real friend. I would lay on the couch and watch Quantum Leap, Highway to Heaven and others for days and weeks at a time. He didn't want kids and he wanted me to have an abortion. I struggled with this greatly. When I believed the baby was going to be stillborn, he got his wish. I don't actually know if this is true or a story I have been telling myself to make it all okay. The guilt and shame I felt was overwhelming. I hated who I was even more. I had secrets. Secrets I never wanted anyone to know about. Secrets that drove my shame even deeper.

Eventually, I let go of the "friends" for a while and moved to another city. I was running from my problems, starting over, and trying to recreate who I thought I needed to be.

I was staying with a friend, a real friend. I didn't recognize the friendship then. I believed it was just another person who pitied my worthless self and was willing to try to "help." I miss her. She did not judge me, and I now know she really had the heart and desire to help me out of my mess. I was not ready for what she was trying to share. If you are out there and you read this, I appreciate everything you tried to do for me.

I loved her and her family. They had their problems, but they worked hard. They had 3 children, and her husband was a really nice guy. I thought to myself, *why can't I find someone like him.* I found myself at the bar more often than I care to admit. Funny story. I didn't even drink. I went on the search for someone new.

That December I found a new "love." We traveled together, I met his friends and family, I learned to salsa dance, and we would go to the rodeo. I really thought this one was different. A few short months later in February, I discovered I was pregnant with baby #4. When I told him I was pregnant, his exact words, "you and that baby will never come before my ex and my other kids." I believed him, I was still a nobody. I packed up my shit and moved to Iowa, where my mother and my sister were at the time. I was determined to be a better human. I knew for this to happen I needed to make some significant changes in my life. Somehow, I just knew that things had to be different. I desperately needed to be a better mother.

In Iowa, I stayed with my sister and her boyfriend for a while. I found a job and started to build my life. "Friends" in this new place managed to find me. I started down that path again and had to make a very conscious decision. I am not doing this again. I moved here to be different, I have a choice and this isn't what I want. I don't know where or when I discover this choice but, I disconnect from them relatively quickly. I can't say I made a lot of better decisions, mostly just different ones. But this one was a biggie.

One thing almost all of my relationships had in common, excluding my saint, was the belief that I could fix them. If I could love them enough, they would be better humans and in turn they would love me and fix what I believed was broken in me. I would be a better human too and live happily ever after.

As you can see, I have had a lot of "love" in my life, even relationships I thought would save me. There are several more that are not included in this book. But real friends were hard to come by, the few I have had in my life are treasures I will never forget. If I have ever called you a friend, and we have lost track of each other, you are in my heart and mind always.

There is value and truth in this lesson Jodi Picoult learned and has passed on that "[a] very wise man once told me that you can't look back—you just have to put the past behind you and find something better in your future."

I wondered as I wandered: was the belief that I could fix them by loving them enough? In turn would they love me and fix what I believed was broken in me?

CHAPTER FOUR – TAKING BACK YOUR POWER

The uphill battle out of the wonder years.

In this chapter, I will share with you the beginning of my journey to take back the power I had lost. You may feel emotions that are scary and uncomfortable but necessary to get back your power. Emotions are the powerhouse to guide you to a happy and balanced life. How you handle your emotions, choices, and behaviors, whether you choose to react or respond, in any event, will lead you away from or back to the goals and desires you have in life. This is where you will start to find your peace, happiness, and sense of belonging.

By now you should have a solid sense that I did not make the best decisions in life. In this chapter we are moving out of the wonder years, these are the days, weeks, months and years that I was just plain ol' Laurie. However, it was during these years that I learned one of the most powerful lessons in life, personal responsibility.

Shortly after moving to Wisconsin my brother and sister-in-law signed me up for a four-day "The Landmark Forum" seminar. Here, I learned about personal responsibility and that it doesn't matter why I made the decisions and choices I did, it just is. I also learned about forgiveness and how to move forward, leaving the past in the rear-view mirror.

"Ice cream; Chocolate or vanilla?" they asked.

"Chocolate." I said, and I mentally ate the chocolate ice cream they were referring to.

Then they asked, "why chocolate?"

I started to justify my answer. And they said, "had you chosen vanilla you could have added the caramel topping."

"I didn't know that!" I said.

"But I chose the chocolate because tastes good, and I like it. The next thing they said changed the way I looked at my past.

Your choices and behaviors, in any event, will lead you away from or back to the goals and desires you have in life.

"The decision was already made; you have already eaten the ice cream; it is too late to change your mind.

Just as you cannot change the decisions you have made in the past. Your decisions were made with the information you had available to you at the time, and you decided, at that time, what was best for you. Right or wrong, good or bad, it is what it is."

You see once you take responsibility for the decisions and choices you have made, you can look at the facts vs the feelings that came afterward. Reliving the story in your mind gives you the opportunity to uncover the hero that made it through a tough decision, situation, or event. You get an opportunity to rewrite the ending.

Life is funny, once you learn the lesson you were meant to learn, it will move you on to the next lesson. If you fail to learn the first time, life will present you with similar situations. Have you ever said, 'why does this keep happening to me?" Well, the answer lies in the lesson.

When you change your mindset to accept what is, you can learn what life is trying to tell you. Remember those speeding tickets? The stories I would tell, *It's not fair! The speed limit should be higher*; or *The cop was having a bad day and wrote me a ticket*; or my personal favorites, *They had a quota to meet* and *I was going downhill!* So, I would blame everyone or everything around me, but refused to take responsibility for speeding. Rewrite the story. Here are the facts: 1) I was speeding, 2) I got caught speeding, and 3) the consequence of my action was a speeding ticket. End of story.

Here are a couple of extreme examples.

In his book *No Hands, No Excuses: Living a No Excuse Life, No Matter What Happens to You*, bestselling author Lee Shelby recaps the story of how he lost both hands in a major electrical accident. As a lineman he was working on a low voltage line, next to a thirteen-thousand-two-hundred-volt electric conductor. The protocol was, when working close to high voltage you must wear the high voltage rubber gloves. He made a choice to ignore that protocol and chose to wear his leather gloves instead. He accidentally touched the conductor and thirteen-thousand-two-hundred-volts of electricity ran through his hands. The bolt cutters he was using exploded, and the electricity burned his hands so severely they had to amputate. He could have blamed the company for not enforcing the protocol, he could have blamed himself and stopped living life, but he took responsibility for his choices. This is an amazing book and I highly recommend reading his full story.

Another example: A friend was in a boating accident. One boat was not following the rules of the no wake zone and the wake tipped the boat he was in. He almost drowned. For years he would not get into a boat. At first, he blamed the other boater for not following the rules of the no wake zone, but when he looked at the facts, he realized his choices led to the near drowning. The story: Because the other boater did not follow the rules I almost died. Observation: it was hot and uncomfortable, and I was a good swimmer, that day I chose not to wear a life jacket. When the boat tipped, I fell out and almost drowned. Facts: the boat created wake in a no wake zone, I fell off the boat, I was not wearing a life jacket, and I almost drowned. He could have made a different choice that day. The lesson: wear a life jacket, even if it is hot and uncomfortable. It's the law.

These are just two examples of taking responsibility and learning how to move forward in life. Both individuals could have made the choice to be afraid and stop reaching for their goals. They could have lived in shame, blame, regret and/or fear and let the rest of their lives pass them by. But they didn't. They looked deep within, unveiled the dominant emotions and decided to rewrite their stories.

10 years after moving to Wisconsin, 10+ years of being "clean" I started my career working with a large financial firm in the corporate office. My second major achievement since the wonder years. They called me and asked me to apply! I had been working as an advisor for another financial firm, but failed! Again, FAIL = First Attempt In Learning.

I did not like playing with other people's money. I did not have the confidence and it showed. However, I was thriving in the corporate world. I loved solving problems, being creative and coming up with new ideas. Most of all I loved working with the clients and advisors and building relationships. Within the first six months, I had been promoted from a front-line agent to an expert. After a year I was promoted again to a coach. Here is where I started to learn the value of leadership. More leadership stories to come when we go back to the wolves.

I had set a goal to become a team leader. I did all the things. I became Kaizen certified. I completed the leadership 360 program and I was charging forward. I didn't get the promotion. I kept trying. I created new training programs, I built rapport with my coworkers and the advisors I worked with. I was awesome or so I thought. Another team leader position opened. I applied again. I didn't get the job. This time, I was angry, heartbroken, sad, frustrated. I didn't understand. I kept thinking, "**what is wrong with me**? This rejection hurts." I had worked so hard. However, I had a great leader at the time. This would be the first time I would recognize what whole-hearted leadership looked like.

She sat me down and explained to me why I didn't get the promotion. She was kind but honest. "You have low self-confidence and you are too emotional," she said. She was right. I would cry at the drop of a hat. I would get angry and walk away or I would just give up. When someone challenged me or my ideas, I would bow my head in shame and give in to their ideas.

Even though I had the technical skills, I did not have the emotional intelligence or the confidence to be a great leader. I did not believe in myself or my potential.

I took that information, and I made a decision to do something about it. I picked up my first book in years. *Emotional Intelligence* 2.0 by Travis Bradberry & Jean Greaves. This was the beginning of a new era. I learned the four core EQ skills: self-awareness, self-management, social awareness, and relationship management; and how to apply them in my life. Needless to say, when I initially took the assessment, I had a lot of work to do.

I started with understanding myself and increasing my self-awareness. Why would I cry so easily? I looked for strategies to help me control the desire to weep in my cubicle. Peppermint essential oils work great, by the way.

Once I mastered the tears, I moved forward to the anger and fear that would cause me to walk away from a conversation. In another book I read, I learned, anger is a sign that you feel mistreated, treated unfairly or a moral dilemma has presented itself. I started expressing myself in a way that would build trust with my co-workers and my boss and my confidence started to grow. I learned how to communicate a little better. A few years later I was promoted to a team called

Platinum Partners. Best career move ever! Initiated by the worst leader ever! I'll tell you that story a little later.

Emotions are not good or bad, they are high and low, and we have them for a purpose. Our emotions try to tell us when something is wrong, when something feels right or when we need more information.

Have you ever had the gut feeling that something just seemed off? Those feelings are guiding your intuition, telling you to be aware or seek more information.

Have you ever been so stricken by someone you felt flutters in your stomach? Those could be your feelings telling you to give it a shot or you need to walk away NOW.

Our feelings have a purpose. To understand that purpose you need to understand and trust your feelings and your intuition. There is so much to learn when it comes to feelings, emotions, intuition, and energy that I will only touch the surface. I am definitely not an expert in this area. I encourage you to explore these topics more in depth.

The hard stuff. Do your feelings and emotions control you and your behavior? If you have trouble maintaining relationships, keeping a job or getting the next promotion. The answer is probably yes.

Have you ever made the statement, *I am the way I am, just deal with it?* or *This is how I have always been*.

Now, I ask of you, how is that working for you?

My guess is, if you have picked up this book, and you have read this far, it's probably not working out in your favor. So, with that in mind how do you start to make the necessary changes?

If you have ever attended an anger management class, one technique they stress is giving yourself time. Walk away, move to another room, walk around the block, breathe, or count to 10. These are strategies that give you the space between reacting or responding to a given situation.

Susan David, PhD, in her book *Emotional Agility*, described a capacity of emotional agility as "loosening up, calming down, and living with more intention. It's about choosing how you'll respond to your emotional warning system. Between stimulus and response there is a space. In that space is our power to choose our response. In our response lies our growth and our freedom."

Once you realize you have the freedom to choose how you will respond to a situation, life gets better. This is a skill that can be learned. Practicing the skills to recognize your feelings and emotions and understanding the underlying meaning within them will help guide your decisions. You can feel the confidence rising inside of you. People will look at you differently. There is a respect that comes with the ability to respond to a situation with integrity, confidence and grace.

Does this mean you will always respond in a favorable manner? No, there will still be times when you react to a situation instead of responding. What it means is you have an opportunity to reflect on what happened.

Take a moment to reflect on a conversation or a situation where you reacted. How did you feel afterwards? Did you feel bad about the words you used or a behavior that was not a reflection of who you are or who you want to be? Take the opportunity to apologize. You may say something like, "You know that conversation we had the other day? I have had an opportunity to think about what I said, and I wanted to apologize. I believe I reacted out of character and I know that if I had taken a minute to think about it, I would have behaved differently. I'm sorry."

What happens when we take ownership of our words and actions? People start to trust you.

Have you ever heard of the marble jar? Brené Brown, one of my most favorite authors, describes it in her book, *Daring Greatly*. Brené tells the story of her daughter's third grade teacher. The gist of the story is people earn trust with small everyday actions. Such as keeping information that is not yours to share confidential, acts of kindness, listening, being present and admitting when you are wrong. We will talk more about trust in another chapter. But know that building trust happens daily.

In Brené Brown's book, *Atlas of the Heart*, she breaks down the many emotions that present themselves on a regular basis. The ability to recognize and define the emotions you are feeling will help you sort through the facts and make a conscious decision to help guide you in the right direction.

Your emotions and feelings are stinkers, they feed off past memories and experiences and often convince you to make quick, emotional and irrational decisions. When you can see your feelings for what they are, a warning system, you can decide if those feelings are telling you the truth, or if you are reacting based on a historical event.

For years I would get upset, not just upset but physically ill and depending on the tone you could see me start to shake when anyone would use foul language. I didn't like it, it made me uncomfortable and very irritable. As I was working through my self-limiting beliefs, I asked myself one day, why was I so caught up in these words. What is it that causes me to react so viscerally? I could feel my heart racing, and my blood pressure skyrocketing. Then the memory hit me like a freight train.

When I was in the 4th grade, I had just started a new school, again. I didn't have any friends and one girl was a real bully. One day we had a substitute teacher. She told the teacher I had called her a bitch. I didn't even know what the word meant, let alone how to use it. However, I got in trouble and had to sit in the front of the room with the teacher, while all the kids stared at me. I was being punished for something I did not do. I was crying uncontrollably, I was embarrassed, I was living in a shame storm created by someone else. (I still bought her candy and tried to be her friend.)

Once I realized I was reacting to feelings and emotions from the past I was able to recreate the ending of that story. I made it through middle school. No one ever really talked about what happened. I still made a few friends. It wasn't that big of a deal, now that I think about it. It was one moment in one day of my life that had created so much angst and anxiety throughout my life.

Do you remember earlier in the chapter, the story about why I did not get the leadership role? I was too emotional. I would cry at the drop of a hat. More often than not, it was someone swearing at me that would send me into a complete meltdown. That is the power your feelings and emotions can have. Once you gain control over your emotions, you will find it is easier to love who you are.

Gaining control over your emotions is a process. You cannot go from despair to elation, or sadness to happiness in one fell swoop. To gain control of your emotions it is important to take one step at a time. If you are feeling depressed, perhaps the next step is to move into sadness, then from sadness into disappointment, disappointment to acceptance and so on. As you progress with each step you gain clarity.

The following diagram is an example of moving from one feeling to another. The feelings you choose may be different, but the idea is the same. Take your emotions up one step at a time.

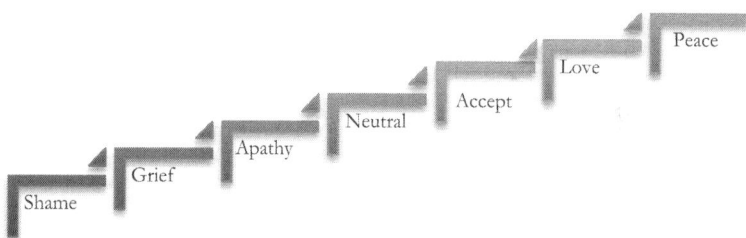

Peace

Love

Accept

Neutral

Apathy

Grief

Shame

CHAPTER FIVE – YOU DON'T HAVE TO FIT IN TO BELONG

Have you ever done something completely against your nature, to impress someone or get them to like you? I have many times throughout my life. In my tween years I would steal change from my parents' change jar so I could buy candy to give out to the other kids. I was desperate for someone to like me. Later in life, I would give in to the intimate desires of others so they would love me. I used my body to get the attention and belonging I thought would make me happy.

The desire to "fit in" is a primal function of life. You want to be liked. You feel important when people want to be around you. You will often behave in ways that you normally wouldn't if it meant getting the attention of others and fitting in.

You don't have to fit in to belong.

Let's talk about authenticity, you don't have to fit in to belong. You will learn how to be your best self and believe in the decisions and choices you make. Mistakes are just decisions where you didn't like the outcome. You will learn what self-forgiveness is and how to leave your past in the rearview mirror.

I saw this somewhere on goodreads.com Sue Fitzmaurice, a nurse, business owner, management consultant and CEO, defines authenticity "to be more concerned with truth than opinions, to be sincere and not pretend, to be free from hypocrisy — 'walk your talk,' to know who you are and to be that person, to not fear others seeing your vulnerabilities, being confident to walk away from situations where you can't be yourself, being awake to your own feelings, being free from others' opinions of you, accepting and loving yourself."

A friend, Linda Sullivan, said, "I have so lost myself in my children's and grandchildren's' lives that I have totally lost who I am. Actually, the truth is I've never known who I am, but I hadn't really felt a need to know until I was no longer needed."

This really hit home to me. Even as I write this book, finding out who I am is a challenge. I was always the mother, the friend, the wife, and now the grandma. I defined myself by who I loved.

What is authenticity? I thought I knew the answer to this question but as I started working to become a better version of myself, I realized I was not even close. I used to believe authenticity was just taking off the mask, but how do you do that when you don't know or like who you are underneath? Authenticity is about knowing why you believe what you do, knowing your values and living them.

In *The Gifts of Imperfection*, Brené Brown says authenticity is an antidote to shame. She defines authenticity as "a collection of choices that we have to make every day. It's about the choice to show up and be real. The choice to be honest. The choice to let our true selves be seen."

To be authentic it's important to define your values. I didn't understand what values meant. Something of value was determined by its worth and I had very little self-worth so how could I base my decisions on values?

Values are your principles, beliefs or behaviors; what you believe is important in life. Let's break this down a little further.

According to Merriam-Webster's dictionary, principles are a general or basic truth on which other truths or theories can be based.

Belief is a state or habit of mind in which trust or confidence is placed in some person or thing.

Behaviors are the way in which someone conducts oneself or behaves.

Here's the catch, your principles are based on your values, your beliefs are based on your values, and your behaviors are based on your values. So what are your values? What do you believe is important in your life? For me, prior to my personal growth journey, my perceived values were: doing whatever was necessary to make other people happy, building confidence in other people at the expense of my own, loving others so they would find their value in the world.

John Maxwell says in *The 15 Invaluable Laws of Growth,* "[i]f you put a small value on yourself, rest assured the world will not raise the price."

Now that I understand values better, my primary values are: Integrity, Faith, Courage, Growth and Family. As I come to a crossroad or I have a big decision to make, I write down my values and ask myself: *Which decision will align best with my values? If I choose this option, am I living inside my integrity? Does this align with my faith? Am I choosing courage? Will this help in my personal growth? And how does this impact my family?*

There will be times when multiple choices align with your values and you will have to choose which one fits best and will help you achieve your goals.

See Appendix for a list of values and complete the exercise in identifying your values.

Your values are the lifeline between you and your goals. When you base your decisions on your values you can put boundaries into place to help guide you in your journey to loving you.

What are Boundaries?

Boundaries are the arbitrary lines we draw in the sand. Some of us don't have them. It's hard to say no when someone needs you and you believe it is your duty or even life purpose to care for them. It's difficult to express your true feelings when it doesn't seem to suit someone else's story or you believe if you say no you may hurt their feelings. It's daunting to stand up for yourself when you believe you are not worth it.

I see a lot of relevant quotes from Adam Grant and one of my favorites is "[b]eing a nice person is about courtesy; you're friendly, polite, agreeable, and accommodating. When people believe they have to be nice in order to give, they fail to set boundaries, rarely say no, and become pushovers, letting others walk all over them."

According to Hazelden Betty Ford Foundation in an article about setting boundaries in addiction, "[p]ersonal boundaries are physical and/or emotional limits that people set for themselves as a way to safeguard their overall well-being.

"Healthy boundaries help people define who they are as a way to ensure relationships are safe, supportive and respectful.

"Unhealthy boundaries are thoughts or behaviors used as a means to manipulate or control relationships to keep people away.

Rokelle Lerner, a popular speaker and trainer on family dynamics, codependency and addiction recovery, captures the meaning of boundaries in this simple statement: "What I value I will protect, but what you value I will respect." In her book, *The Object of My Affection Is in My Reflection: Coping with Narcissists* she lays out her persona bill of rights:

"PERSONAL BILL OF RIGHTS FOR MY RELATIONSHIPS

1. I have a right to be treated with courtesy and respect.
2. I have a right to be the only romantic or sexual interest in my partner's life.
3. I have a right to be informed about our assets, manage my own finances, and choose how I spend my money.
4. I have a right to have a say in decisions that affect myself and my family.
5. I have a right to be wrong and make mistakes without being punished or humiliated.
6. I have the right to live without emotional or physical violence.
7. I have the right to voice my opinion respectfully without retribution.

8. I have the right to have my personal property treated with respect.
9. I have the right to talk to others about matters that affect me.
10. I have the right to choose my own friends.
11. I have the right to enjoy myself.
12. I have the right to live without guns or pornography in my house.
13. My children have the right to be treated with respect and dignity."
(Adapted from Cooper & Cooper, 2008)

These are Rokelle Lerners personal bill of rights for her relationships. What does your bill of rights look like?

Establishing boundaries can be hard, especially when you haven't had any in the past. You believe it will distance you from the people who are essential to your daily life. However, what you will find by setting boundaries is those who care for and love you will accept those boundaries, those who don't will get angry, dismissive and try to shame you. When that doesn't work, they will move on to another victim who will allow them to manipulate and control their environment.

To be honest, I still struggle with setting boundaries. I work at it daily by asking myself, *Is this what I need today? Will this help or hinder my goals? Do I want to say yes? Does this align with my values?*

It is easy to overbook your day agreeing to do all the things with all the people. When you choose to not set boundaries you can become overwhelmed causing stress, anxiety, and feelings of failure when you cannot meet the needs of everyone all the time. Setting boundaries gives you peace of mind, a chance to take a deep breath and relax when your body and mind are maxed out.

How do you know if you need to set boundaries? Here are a few things to look for:

- You are what other people want/need you to be
- You are afraid to stand up for yourself
- You give too much of your time.
- You say "yes" when you really want to say "no"
- You feel guilty for taking time to yourself.
- You feel used by others.
- You have toxic relationships.
- You make too many personal sacrifices.
- You feel guilty when others aren't happy.

- You worry about what others think of you.

My sister is a great example of learning to set boundaries. She was always torn between tasks, family, friends, and work. Having a special needs daughter, her schedule was entirely dependent on whether her daughter could handle the event or if she had a nurse or caretaker for the day. She was constantly running around trying to get things done with the little time she had while her daughter was in school or with a caretaker. She would worry about what she forgot, she was anxious about what other people might say or think about her life and how she raised her daughter. She felt guilty for not being everywhere all the time. She was exhausted.

Over the past few years, she has learned to set boundaries. She says no when it really isn't feasible, or it is just too much for that day. She works hard to make time for friends and family, but she has learned to take care of herself first. Sometimes that means a little downtime. Recently she sold a business she owned—it was a big step to living her best life. She has had to let go of toxic relationships, that was one of the hardest things she had to face in the not-so-distant past. She is an amazing example of learning how to set boundaries.

A friend and business coach, Jenny Fields, had this to say about boundaries, "Not setting boundaries can make life feel like a never-ending shitshow. You're constantly getting taken advantage of, feeling drained, and not getting your needs met. It's like being a doormat; constantly being walked all over by others. But when you choose to set boundaries, it's like a weight has been lifted off your shoulders. You're no longer a pushover, and you can finally start taking care of yourself. Your relationships improve, you have more energy, and overall, life just feels more fun. It's like you've reclaimed your power and can finally start living life on your own terms."

Self-forgiveness

Forgive and forget, I have heard this my whole life. It seems easy enough. How do you forgive someone who cheated on you and forget? You don't. You carry that broken trust and fear into your next relationship.

How do you forgive and forget when you have been hurt by someone you trusted? You may be able to forgive, but can you ever really forget?

When Charlie hurt me, it was hard to forgive let alone forget. I was so angry. The fear that another man would hurt me was unimaginable. Yes, I dated other guys, but one of the reasons none of them worked was because I didn't trust them. They hadn't given me any reason not to. But my past experiences tainted the relationship before it even had a chance. It took over 10 years before I found someone that I felt comfortable with and another 2 years before that someone was able to get near my face without me flinching. I married him. We have been married now for 9 years. I had to forgive myself as much as I needed to forgive Charlie. However, I didn't forget, I learned.

When I sent my daughter to live with her dad, when I left my son because I felt he was better off without me, when I decided to end it all, each of these events in my life left me feeling worthless. I believed I was a horrible person. How could I possibly forgive myself for the horrible person I had become?

Forgive by definition is to stop feeling angry or resentful toward (someone) for an offense, flaw, or mistake.

Stop feeling angry or resentful. Read that again.

It didn't say make amends, it didn't say to accept them back into your life. It said, stop feeling angry or resentful. This is a choice.

Actress Patty Duke said, "[i]t's toughest to forgive ourselves. So it's probably best to start with other people. It's almost like peeling an onion. Layer by layer, forgiving others, you really do get to this point where you can forgive yourself."

So how do you forgive yourself? What has happened that caused you to feel angry or resentful? What decisions did you make? Accept what is. You cannot change the past. Being angry and resentful toward yourself will not help you or any other person.

The choice is yours. You can stay in your anger and what you will find you attract is more anger. You can choose to remain resentful, and you will find more resentment. If you choose to forgive, you will find forgiveness. This is the law of attraction. It is real. Forgive.

Forget? You don't forget, you learn. Once you learn then you can move beyond the debilitating emotions that caused you so much fear and anxiety.

How do you become the person you want to be? One step at a time. One event at a time. Don't try to fix everything all at once. Small steps everyday will help you make the changes you want in your life. Forgiving yourself for the mistakes you have made is a great first step. Remember, every choice or decision you made was made with the information you had at the time. It was what you believed you needed to get through the day or a tough situation. Forgive and learn.

Chapter Six – Back to the Wolves

This will be the beginning of whole-hearted leadership in your personal and professional life. What is whole-hearted leadership? How does it impact your life and those around you? How can you be the best leader in your life?

What is whole-hearted leadership? It is showing kindness when you want to punch someone, it is exhibiting empathy when you want to judge them. Whole-hearted leadership is building strong relationships through trust, communication, and respect.

When I was working for a financial company, I experienced different leadership styles. One stands out as the worst ever and two who inspired me to be the best leader I could be.

Let me tell you another story. I had a great position with great benefits, 5 weeks paid vacation and excellent pay. I enjoyed my job. At first. However, I stopped "showing up" when I believed my leader did not believe in me. Every day I physically went to work, but my mind was always somewhere else. I felt I couldn't get any better, I was sitting stagnant doing just what I had to, to get through the day.

I dreamed of the day that Faith, my previous leader, would show up again. She was awesome, she believed in me more than I believed in myself. She believed I had more potential and that I could achieve more than what I was doing and I wanted to prove her RIGHT. However, she had moved on to bigger and better things and this new "leader" took her place. The new "leader" did not see my potential, I felt she had a chip on her shoulder, I would have sworn she had something against me. She discouraged me regularly pointing out all the things I did wrong and ignored all of the things I did right. She didn't try to coach me to be better, she didn't help me understand what I could do to improve my work. I really believed she didn't want me there.

That is when I discovered the power of leadership and influence. Because of her, I found a new opportunity and moved on to a new team. That "leader" lost half her team within 6 months before she was moved into another position within the company.

A leader in title only, will discourage and belittle others. The fear of someone taking their title, drives them to focus on the negative.

Do you want to be like Faith, believing in the potential of yourself and others or the new leader...? This applies to leading yourself. How do you talk to yourself? Are you encouraging? Do you consistently point out all your flaws and negative traits? Do you focus on what you do well or dwell on the areas in which you fail? Self-talk is critical in leading yourself. It's not a bunch of fancy woo-woo. Would you talk to your friends, your children or your spouse the way you talk to yourself? If the answer is, HELL NO, then you need to work on loving you. And that is why we are here.

In the story about the wolves, they claim the first group are the weak or the sick, they are said to set the pace for the rest of the group. This is just a story. You may have experienced the leaders who lead from the front, they are perceived as the strongest and have the experience to oversee what is happening in the company. However, in real life many leaders/parents believe they are there to dictate what should be done, to monitor, review and correct you when you are not doing something right. A true leader leads with encouragement, belief and empathy. They are trudging the path to success so others can follow more easily.

> *No one has the right to lead your life except you.*

Perhaps you don't consider yourself as a leader in your relationship, that doesn't mean you cannot be a strong leader in your life. No one has the right to lead your life except you. I'm not saying you need to be a hard ass. I'm saying take back your power to make a difference and lead your life on your terms.

"When you focus on problems, you will have more problems; when you focus on possibilities you will have more opportunities," wrote Zig Ziglar in how leaders shape themselves and the people and world around them.

As I mentioned in the beginning, a quote from John Maxwell, "leadership is influence, nothing more, nothing less." If you are influencing people daily, good or bad, you are a leader, right? So how do you become the best leader you can be?

Relationships built on a foundation of effective communication, respect and trust will stand strong through the trials and errors of life.

Let's start with an acronym I started using in 2021: CLEAR. It is easy to remember, and it gives the five main aspects of becoming a wholehearted leader in your life, both personal and professional. The same acronym is also used by John Maxwell, but trademarked C.L.E.A.R Leadership: C for Communication; L for Leadership; E for Equipping; A for Attitude, (we both agree attitude is critical in life and in leadership); and R for Relationships. I love John Maxwell and his path of servant leadership. I highly recommend any of his programs.

Let's look at the CLEAR I use and elaborate on each of the five main aspects of becoming a wholehearted leader. I really started focusing on these aspects of life when my son tried to take his life and I started to focus on rebuilding the broken relationships with my children. What I have discovered is this works in almost every aspect of life.

> C – Cultivate empathy
> L – Lean into curiosity and vulnerability
> E – Effective listening

A – Attitude is everything
R – Respect and values

Cultivate Empathy

"Empathy has no script. There is no right or wrong way to do it. It's simply listening, holding space, withholding judgement, emotionally connecting, and communicating that incredibly healing message of 'You're not alone,'" wrote Brené Brown.

How do you define empathy? Cognitive empathy refers to our ability to identify and understand other peoples' emotions.

There are major differences between empathy, sympathy and compassion. Empathy is to be other minded. It is the ability to recognize the feelings and emotions in others without taking away or justifying their feelings and emotions.

Sympathy is to feel sorry for someone.

I lived my life with compassion. Compassion is an attempt to absorb the pain others are experiencing and try to take their pain away from them. You cannot take away someone else's pain, if you try you will only diminish the feelings they are having and cause yourself more harm than you are doing good.

I believed if I could take their pain away, their lives would be better. I have learned that we each experience feelings and emotions differently. The loss of a loved one is painful, where the loss of a pet is just as painful for someone else. Empathy does not compare the two. The emotions or feelings are the same. Empathy is the ability to accept where they are and not judge or compare how much better or worse your pain is or was.

Their feelings are theirs; it is there to help them learn and grow. Walk beside them, support them, and love them through it. That is empathy.

Lean into Curiosity and Vulnerability

As children you used to ask why all the time. You were looking to understand the world around you. You were learning. There was no fear of judgment when you were young. As you get older, you fear what others think of you. You worry about sounding stupid, or fear asking questions that others deem ignorant. So, you keep quiet. Curiosity takes a back seat and you lose the creative, wonderful, exciting wonder around you. **Get curious, ask questions, seek to understand.**

Vulnerability, as I mentioned earlier, is a strength, not a weakness!

Brené Brown defines vulnerability as "uncertainty, risk, and emotional exposure. But vulnerability is not weakness; it's our most accurate measure of courage…. Vulnerability is not winning or losing; it's having the courage to show up and be seen when we have no control over the outcome. Vulnerability is not weakness; it's our greatest measure of courage. People who wade into discomfort and vulnerability and tell the truth about their stories are the real badasses."

Vulnerability is the ability to admit when you are wrong or when you have made a decision where you didn't like the outcome. Vulnerability builds trust!

When I started rebuilding the relationships with my children, I had to be vulnerable. It was hard to admit the mistakes that I had made and to address the failure I had been as their mother. Having heartfelt, honest conversations about where I was at different points in my life, slowly started to build trust. It has taken a fair amount of time, but I have a good relationship with my children and it continues to get better.

Effective Listening

"You're not listening to me!" Have you ever heard these words from your spouse, children, friends, or co-workers? You feel that you have heard them, you listened to their words, but your personal and professional relationships are still rocky.

Most people will agree that listening is the most important aspect of any relationship. Without it there are misunderstandings, poor communication, and broken trust. If you were to ask anyone if they are a good listener, the answer would be a resounding yes. The truth is only about 26% of people actually listen effectively. What does it mean to listen, I mean really listen? Here are a few tips to help improve your listening skills.

- Sit facing the person you are communicating with; your body language says more than you think.
- Be attentive, turn off your phone and give them your undivided attention.
- DON'T interrupt. It is easy to try and interject, our brains are already processing and creating a

response before they have even finished the sentence.

- Repeat in your own words what you believe they are saying. Don't just regurgitate their words.
- Ask questions. This is what I am hearing, does that sound right, or is that what you are trying to say. This gives them a chance to confirm or correct without judgment.

When you take the time to listen, you build trust. Trust creates strong relationships. Strong relationships fulfill your need for belonging.

Listening is one of the more difficult aspects to master. Your brain processes information far quicker than a person can speak, so your mind is already forming the end of their sentence and generating a response. When I was listening to my children as we worked on our relationships, it was really hard to listen to their feelings, emotions, and the hurt that I had cultivated in their lives. My mind jumped directly to justification and self-defense. Listening to understand is different than hearing the words that are being said.

Attitude is Everything

In psychology, an attitude refers to a set of emotions, beliefs, and behaviors toward a particular object, person, thing, or event. Attitudes are often the result of experience or upbringing, and they can have a powerful influence over behavior. While attitudes are enduring, they can also change. Your attitude creates energy. Your attitude, when entering any type of interaction, also makes a difference. I have a sign on my door leaving the house that reads, Check your attitude at the door and exit with a smile. This reminds me every day to check in with my emotions and choose to start my day with a positive attitude. When you enter into a conversation or interaction of any type with a bad attitude, 1) you will not listen effectively, 2) you will judge the person unfairly, and 3) the conversation will end poorly. Breaking trust.

Picture this: you get out of bed, take a shower, and grab a cup of coffee. It's a beautiful day and starts off amazingly. You leave for work early, the sun is shining, birds are

When you choose to enter a conversation with curiosity, vulnerability, and a positive attitude the end result will be a stronger relationship built on trust.

chirping, and you think to yourself, *Today is going to be a great day!*

Halfway to work someone cuts you off (they didn't see you) and you slammed on your brakes and spilled coffee down the front of your clean white shirt. The sun is still shining, and the birds are still chirping, but now you need coffee and a clean shirt. How is your attitude now?

You are running a bit behind, but you make the decision to stop at your favorite coffee shop to get a fresh cup of joe. They are busier than usual, but you really want that coffee so you wait. The lady in front of you is indecisive and seems to take forever, you just want her to move out of your way. The clock is ticking. How is your attitude now?

Finally, you get your coffee, get in the car only to discover your order is wrong. How's your attitude now?

You storm back into the coffee shop and start yelling at the young lady behind the register. It's not her fault, she didn't make the coffee, but she is the one who felt your wrath.

People make mistakes. Yes, even you.

Will you allow this to ruin your entire day? Will you be the reason someone else has a bad day? Are you going to be cranky all day with coworkers or complete strangers who had nothing to do with your morning struggles?

The choice is yours. Every minute of every day you have a choice. This happened to me. I was the barista, I have also been on the giving end and it did not feel great.

When you choose to enter a conversation with curiosity, vulnerability, and a positive attitude, the end result will be a stronger relationship built on trust.

Respect and Values

I believe there are two levels of respect. Respect that is given and respect that is earned.

Respect Given: A level of respect that people tend to forget about. It's the level of courtesy that you give other people, simply because you recognize that they are human. We all have blood running through our veins. We all have our demons. Not everyone has to automatically have your admiration without working for it, but everyone deserves basic human courtesy.

<u>Respect Earned</u>: A more common meaning that you earn respect from others, essentially proving your worth. This is true when we think of respect in terms of admiration for someone, their personal character, their values, or their work. Examples of respect earned would be Mother Teresa or Mahatma Gandhi. I had this level of respect for the leader who sat me down and explained to me why I didn't get that leadership position.

<u>Values</u>: Values are your principles, beliefs or behaviors; what you believe is important in life. We talked about values and their importance in an earlier chapter. When you communicate with your values in mind, your conversations will have greater meaning, depth and integrity. When you share your values with others they gain a greater understanding of who you are and what is important to you.

Relationships are built on communication, trust, and respect. Trust and respect are built on how you choose to communicate. Just like a 3-legged stool with only one or two legs the chair

will be unstable and fall and so will your relationships.

I know this from personal experience. When I met my now husband. I did not

I was wrong. It was me. I needed to change.

know how to communicate effectively. I could talk, I used my words, but I didn't know how to build a solid connection through communication. The first several years were a little more than rocky. In fact in the first 3 years of marriage, I threatened divorce a dozen times or more. Our relationship started with the same idea I had in previous relationships, that I could fix him. Alcohol was our worst enemy. But I was determined not to let this relationship fail.

Trust was broken, many times. He broke my trust with his drinking and I broke his trust with the constant threat of divorce. Respect was almost non-existent. I won't go into a lot of detail here but know that by the 4th year of marriage it was shit or get off the pot! Something had to change and I thought it was all about him. I was wrong. It was me. I needed to change.

My son was 17 years old. It was February and it had been a long, cold, hard winter in Wisconsin and not just because of the temperatures. My relationships with my husband and my son were broken. I didn't understand what was happening. I felt like I was losing everything.

One day, I was fighting with my son to get up and get his butt to school. He refused. This was a regular fight, at least 3 or 4 times a week. I was working from home at this time and I had been down in my office. Angry and frustrated, I walked upstairs to yell at him again. This time, my world crumbled as he yelled back at me, "don't worry about me, I won't be here much longer!" "What do you mean?" I yelled back, "I just took a bunch of Tylenol so I can get out of this world!" he replied. Those may not have been the exact words but, he had decided to end it, all of it. It took my breath away, broke my heart and changed my life and his.

For the next several hours, all I could do was cry uncontrollably. I was terrified I was about to lose my baby, again. Only this time, it was his choice. The next few weeks were a whirlwind of emotions. Anger, fear, frustration, sadness, and despair.

I couldn't understand what he was going through. I loved him with all my heart; all I ever wanted was for him to be happy and successful in life. Where did I go wrong? I realized that in loving him, I had done everything for him—gold stars and smiley stickers just for trying. I had stolen his self-confidence by taking care of the little things, keeping him out of trouble, and solving his problems for him. I didn't give him the opportunity to ask questions, solve his own problems and discover who he was. I inadvertently sent the message that I didn't believe he could do it himself. I was limiting his potential. I was the very definition of a helicopter parent. This is what my husband and I fought about more often than not.

At this point, I made a decision. Something had to change and now! I was angry with myself and my husband. I told him, my son and I are moving home, you can come with us or not, the choice is yours, but things have to change.

They did, we sold our home and moved our family, including my husband's nephew and my mother-in-law, with dementia, to Colorado so I could be close to my sister and we could have the support of my family. This is when I really started looking at myself, hard.

We were fortunate, my son lived to tell his story, and maybe someday he will share his side. This is where I began to understand the value of communication and the importance of building strong relationships. I started to learn what it meant to be a leader in my life.

I began letting my son own the experiences and consequences of his choices and decisions; I stopped "fixing" his mistakes, and I started telling him how much I believed in him, and I listened.

I knew in my heart he had unlimited potential, and I started setting expectations to help move him out of his comfort zone and into his strengths. Today he is a happier 22-year-old, married, and has a child of his own. I thank God every day for getting us through.

It would take another 2 years before I had clarity and 2 more years before I really understood what wholehearted leadership meant in my life. There have been a lot of failures, falls, stumbles, fights, tears, hugs, and laughs to get where we are today.

In this journey we call life, I have never wanted to manage people. I have a desire to lead and love. I lead through support, encouragement, motivation, and empowerment. I lead by helping to overcome self-limiting beliefs and encouraging positive self-esteem. I lead by asking the tough questions and getting great minds together to encourage and create great ideas and empowering solutions.

I don't always know what prevents us from growing into and reaching our full potential. I do know that if we stop growing, we stop living. This game we call life doesn't end until we stop breathing.

P.S. – My husband and I are growing together, stronger, and more intimate than ever as we learn daily how to respect, trust, and communicate together. More to come in a later chapter.

CHAPTER SEVEN – TRUST YOURSELF

Trust, I talk a lot about trust. Building trust with others is important but what is most important is learning how to trust yourself. Let's start by exploring what it looks like when you don't trust yourself.

When you don't trust yourself, your ability to make decisions, your reliability, or your character you give your power to others.

What happens when you don't trust yourself, you feel worthless, anxious, worried. You look to others for advice, you depend on the opinions of those around you and what other people think becomes a life you can't sustain.

In my 30s, I had very little trust in myself or my abilities. Even after completing my associates degree, I didn't trust that I could make a solid decision. I didn't know who I was. I started to mimic other people who I thought had it all together. The good news is I tried new things. The bad news was that I was fake and people could tell.

I became anxious and worried about what everyone else thought about me. Depression would set in and every now and then would decide to stay for a while. There were days I struggled getting out of bed. Showers were completely optional, and I had no interest in doing many of the things I enjoyed.

I would hang out with family and friends, but I just wanted to eat, sleep, and go to work. Parenting was a challenge. I let my son play video games all day, I didn't help with homework, his math assignment made me feel less than adequate and he was only in the 4th grade! We didn't have a lot of money, so we didn't do much together. I gained a lot of weight during this time. I reached 250 pounds thanks to pizza, nachos, and cookies just to name a few. I felt even worse about myself. I didn't like who I was, I didn't like what I looked like, and I hated the person I had become.

After a visit to my sisters, I decided to start making some changes. As we go through the seven aspects of self-trust, we will explore some of the ups and downs I experienced during this process.

First, what is trust really?

The Oxford languages define trust as a firm belief in the reliability, truth, ability, or strength of someone or something. Merriam-webster defines trust as the assured reliance on the character, ability, strength, or truth of someone or something.

We know that strong relationships are built on trust, communication, and respect. That includes your relationship with yourself. How do you learn to trust yourself when you have made so many mistakes?

How do you eat an elephant? One bite at a time.

Building self-trust requires patience, empathy, and grace for who you were and who you are becoming. You will start to gain confidence and trust in yourself as you rewrite your story. Every time you discover the hero in your past and take responsibility for your choices and actions, you will feel your voice returning. Every time you take a step towards the person you want to be you begin to take back your power.

Brené Brown says trust is a seven-letter word. In her book *Dare to Lead* she breaks it down into an acronym B.R.A.V.I.N.G. for building trust with others. We are going to use this same concept for building trust within yourself.

> B – Boundaries
> R – Reliability
> A – Accountability
> V – Vault
> I – Integrity
> N – Nonjudgement
> G – Generosity

Boundaries

We talked about boundaries in an earlier chapter. Boundaries are the arbitrary lines we draw in the sand. It is important to set boundaries, even if they are small ones to start. Each time you set a boundary and stick with it, you build a little more self-trust. It is about being consistent.

Brené Brown said, "[d]aring to set boundaries is about having the courage to love ourselves, even when we risk disappointing others."

I have struggled with setting boundaries for as long as I can remember. I tried starting with the big ones, you know cutting people out of my life because they were mean. Well, they weren't mean all the time and they are one of my few friends that actually talk to me and well maybe that is not a good boundary even though they really were not very nice most of the time.

Oops. Ok that didn't work and felt worse about myself than when I started. I was accepting people in my life when I knew they were not good for me, but I wasn't ready to piss them off completely and let them go. So I decided to start a little smaller. I mentioned earlier a friend where I could only spend about an hour with her. That is a boundary. When I schedule time with her, I make it clear that my time is limited. I was not mean about it. I had tried to talk to her about the negativity, but I didn't really know how back then.

When setting boundaries, it is not a "one size fits all." Boundaries can be specific to a person or event. Just because they're family doesn't mean you have to stay for 5 hours enduring the criticism that accompanies the family gatherings. Say your hellos and graciously bow out of the rest of the event, assuming you feel the need to attend at all.

Start small, as you build your self-trust you will know what feels right, what gives you energy instead of sucking the life out of you. Boundaries do get easier.

Reliability

Take small actions daily, weekly or monthly that you believe you can complete. It could be as simple as putting the dishes away when the dishwasher has finished or wiping the mirror when you finish getting ready in the morning. These small actions build self-reliability. Again, start small.

I didn't, I decided I was going to call my daughter and my dad and talk to my friends every week. What I didn't think about was the time commitment, you can spend a lot of time talking to people and letting other things fall to the wayside. I couldn't maintain my commitment. It added a strain on my relationship with my daughter when I didn't make the calls.

"Reliability is the precondition for trust," said Wolfgang Schauble, a German lawyer. You start with realistic expectations and you make commitments you can keep. You begin to trust what you say to yourself. You begin to believe that when you say you will do something, you actually will. Because you have taken the time, thought it through, and determined that this is important to you, it is something worth your time and effort.

As you follow through, you gain confidence. Trust me, I know it's not easy. When you miss a day, or flake out on a commitment, give yourself grace, and start again. No one is perfect. It's always best to call and cancel. Communication is critical. If you can't, or you don't, be sure to apologize to those who may have been affected by your flake out, which leads us to accountability.

Accountability

We have covered personal accountability in depth, and according to mindtools.com, personal accountability means you take ownership of what happens as a result of your choices and actions. You don't blame others or make excuses, and you do what you can to make amends when things go wrong. To become more accountable, make sure that you're clear about your roles and responsibilities.

Thomas Matt said, "we all have our lives, and the accountability for the achievement of our dreams and goals falls strictly on our own shoulders."

Accountability is a tough one. It sounds easy enough. The truth is it takes work. Daily habits make a difference in building trust within

> *Daily habits make a difference in building trust within yourself.*

yourself. *Atomic Habits* by James Clear is a great resource for implementing small daily habits. "The only way to make progress, the only choice I had, was to start small," Clear wrote.

Vault

This is a big one. Brené Brown says "[y]ou don't share information or experiences that are not yours to share." However, this applies to you personally. This goes right up there with shedding light on shame. You don't have to share everything all the time. Being transparent or vulnerable does not mean you share everything with everyone. Share what is important to you to make a point or build a report. Knowing when, where and why to share is important.

Valerie Plame an American writer, spy novelist, and former Central Intelligence Agency officer. Wrote, "[my] take is, privacy is precious. I think privacy is the last true luxury. To be able to live your life as you choose without having everyone comment on it or know about."

I used to share everything as soon as I would meet someone. I believed I was being authentic and transparent. But the truth was, I was actually driving people away. TMI: Too much information.

Share when the time is right, with the right person and in the right place. This is a skill that can be learned. As I mentioned before, start with someone you trust. For me, it was my therapist, my sister and eventually my husband.

Integrity

I used a quote by Brené Brown earlier and I will use it again because it is so incredibly important. Integrity means "[c]hoosing courage over comfort; choosing what's right over what's fun, fast, or easy; and practicing your values, not just professing them."

Your body will try to warn you when you are stepping out of your integrity. Your heart beats faster, you may start to sweat, you begin to question if you are doing the right thing. Stop and ask yourself, what will keep me inside my integrity. Are the decisions and actions I choose aligned with my values?

"Have the courage to say no. Have the courage to face the truth. Do the right thing because it is right. These are the magic keys to living your life with integrity," wrote W. Clement Stone in *The Success System That Never Fails*.

When I made the decision to focus on my integrity, my life started to change for the better almost immediately. There were times when I would have to apologize for committing to something beforehand that compromised my values or my integrity and believe it or not, people started to respect my boundaries and my choices.

There may be times when you are choosing courage over comfort when you will experience the same feelings. Choosing courage is one of the toughest to stay inside of your integrity. It's easy to avoid conflict. Having a tough conversation with someone you care about, or choosing to say no when you know they are counting on you but the request is crossing a boundary, are examples of choosing courage over comfort.

Practicing your values also builds self-trust. You can say family is important, but if you spend all of your time at work or out shopping with friends you are not aligned with your values and shame starts to rear is ugly head again.

Non-Judgmental

Stop judging and criticizing yourself. Negative self-talk is judging. *I suck at this. I'm not good enough. I will never be smart enough. I am not as pretty as she is.* This is self-judgment. Pay attention when you start to criticize others. Where you judge others is an area of your life that you are prone to shame.

To build self-trust you will need to learn how to overcome what Cathy Reilly calls "the itty-bitty-shitty committee" in her book *Unleash Your Inner Voice.* Another great resource I highly recommend reading to get deeper understanding into overcoming negative self-talk and learning how to ask for help when you need it.

Zoe Ball, British radio presenter, recalled "[s]omeone taught me this really lovely thing, which is when you're panicking or thinking, 'I can't do this, I can't do this,' you just say, 'Right. Hi, negative thoughts. Stop bothering me. If you just wait there, I'm going to do this job, then I'll come back and talk to you later."

Generosity

Be generous with yourself and your heart. You have good qualities, appreciate the amazing person that you are. Give yourself the benefit of the doubt. You are working on you and making the best decisions and choices you can with the information you have available.

Generosity for others was easy. I would give the shirt off my back, the last $5 in my pocket or the food I had for myself to help someone else. Generosity is great. However, to be truly generous you must take care of yourself first. You cannot take care of others if you are too sick, depressed, or dead. Take care of you!

"Generosity is the most natural outward expression of an inner attitude of compassion and loving-kindness," taught The Dalai Lama XIV.

CHAPTER EIGHT – LOVE YOURSELF

Self-love seems selfish, right? In the past few years self-love and self-care have been big buzzwords. The Covid pandemic shed light on a serious deficiency in our society. Maybe you have noticed a shift in the atmosphere. If not, get your head out of the sand. Look around. Your mental health and wellbeing are critical to live a happy, joy filled and successful life. You were not put on earth to walk this journey alone. It's important to learn to ask for help. We are designed to work together.

Self-love is defined by Wikipedia as "love of self" or "regard for one's own happiness or advantage."

Self-care from Oxford languages is defined as the practice of taking action to preserve or improve one's own health. The practice of taking an active role in protecting one's own well-being and happiness, particularly during periods of stress.

Setting boundaries, communicating your wants and needs, asking for help and taking time to relax and renew your spirit are all forms of self-love and self-care.

One of the most critical aspects for self-love is taking care of you. The next is learning to ask for help. And finally accepting that help with grace and gratitude.

Taking care of you is about small simple tasks that make you feel great. Let's get started on the small simple steps for self-care.

You will experience ups and downs. When I was at my lowest points in life I stopped taking care of myself. Once I recognized I was in a depression there were a few things I would do to help pull myself out. Here are a few examples of self-care that you can use when you are feeling low.

1. Take a shower, cry if you need to. Wash away the yuks.
2. Put on some lotion. I like the smell good ones. The scents, especially citrus, peppermint, wintergreen, and lavender, ignite endorphins and help lift the spirit.
3. Turn on some happy music. I have a playlist of songs that I love just for these moments in life.
4. Dance, start your day with a short happy dance. This also releases the feel-good endorphins.

5. Declutter your home or living space. When your space is dirty or cluttered, so is your brain.

6. Get back to nature. Fresh air and sunshine always help me feel better. I can use the time to relax or reflect on areas I want to improve.

7. Read a book. I have several self-help books, fantasy and other fiction and nonfiction books I love to curl up with. It helps take my mind to another dimension where I can get away.

8. Get your hair and/or nails done if the budget allows, don't make yourself feel guilty for spending money you don't have. Get together with a friend and make your own spa day at home.

9. Breathe. Take time, even just a few minutes for deep breaths. The extra oxygen aids in relaxation and helps to clear the mind.

These are just a few examples I like to use. Remember, start small. I have learned to try and incorporate these into my daily life. It helps prevent the lows before they can start. Mark Twain stated, "[t]he secret of getting ahead is getting started. The secret to getting started is breaking your overwhelming tasks into small manageable tasks, and then starting on the first one."

Communicating your wants and needs. I know what you're thinking. No one wants to hear what you want or need. If you ask people for what you want you're self-absorbed, if you ask for what you need, you're needy. The problem isn't that you are self-absorbed or needy. The problem is that you don't believe you are worth what you want and need. You are worth it. You are learning how to communicate and build strong relationships. Now let's talk about how to communicate your wants and needs.

Andre Gide advised, "[t]he most important things to say are those which often I did not think necessary for me to say—because they were too obvious."

Let me start by saying that beating around the bush, dropping hints or being the martyr will get you nowhere. I'm sure I am not alone here in saying I've done all of those things and none of them worked. Ever.

Dr. Margie Warrell says in her revised book *Stop Playing Safe:*, "[t]hink about what your ideal outcome would be and then confidently, courageously, ask for it. Not in an entitled way. Not in an aggressive way. But in a way that conveys that you know your worth."

Gary Chapman in *The Five Love Languages* said, "[v]erbal communication is essential in order to understand what is going on inside other people. If they do not tell us their thoughts, their feelings, and their experiences, we are left to guess."

You often have hidden expectations. Those ideas you create in your mind of what the perfect date night, quiet time, a day at the beach or the family vacation would look like, but you don't share that information with your significant others, family, or friends. It's important to ask yourself, *what are my expectations? What am I really looking for? Are my expectations realistic?* This will help you to be clear in what you are asking for.

When my husband and I would go out I expected that when we got home we would have "fun." However, his expectations were going out, having a few drinks. Then come home. After a few drinks "fun" isn't going to happen. Once I was clear in my expectations and we were on the same page, life got a lot less complicated. Be clear in your expectations.

Finally, you don't always get what you want. Don't take it personally. Respond with grace and move on.

Remember your fears and insecurities will try to tell you they rejected your request because…insert story. It's not true. If you were to ask them, I'm sure there is a valid, logical reason and even if there is not a valid reason, it is about them, not you.

Ask for help!

Asking for help can be hard, but I am going to share with you how asking for help is actually helping others.

I mentioned earlier that you were not put on this planet to travel alone. As humans we have been designed to work together. Often, we fail to ask for help for 4 main reasons.

- You don't want to be seen as weak or unable to complete a task
- You're a perfectionist
- You feel shame
- You feel a loss of control

First, it's ok to let go of control. Your strengths are someone else's weakness and your weakness is someone else's strength. In our society today, asking for help is often equal to not being enough. It has been ingrained in you since you were a child to pick yourself up and be independent. "I don't need you, I can do it myself," says my 2-year-old grandson.

It is actually beneficial for us to reach out for help. Doing so can release us from the belief we have that we have to be okay all the time. "It's okay not to be okay."

When I started dating my husband, I realized I might have been a little bit of a control freak. I wouldn't ask for help. We had been together for about 2 years and we were taking a road trip to see my daughter. I had experienced some terrifying drivers and refused to let him drive. I had trust issues. However, I was exhausted, and I needed help. I had a choice, I could pull over and rest for the night, which would delay our arrival, or I could ask for help. I finally asked him to take the wheel. I did not sleep. Every bump in the road I was startled. It took time but eventually I learned to trust his driving and he took the wheel a little more often. Now he drives most of the time, it's like I have my own chauffeur.

Sometimes, we need to let go of control. Believe me when I say, it's well worth it. Asking for help compromises our ego's. However, by asking for help, we build trust and create stronger relationships.

By not asking for help you increase your levels of frustration and stress, you feel overwhelmed, indecisive, and can derail your timeline. Not only are you wasting time, but the stress is taking a toll on your physical and mental health and as a result, you're forced to come to a complete halt.

What are you saying to others when you ask for help? You value their opinion, talent, and skills, which will help you build connections, community, and trust.

Finally, it's important to accept help with grace and gratitude. When someone offers to help, it does not mean they are looking down on you, or believe you are incapable of doing for yourself. When genuine help is offered, it says I love or care about you.

Often when people offer to help, you fear there is an ulterior motive. There is an unspoken expectation of reciprocation. If I accept help from you in turn you will expect me to offer to help you, and I don't believe I can provide the same level of help. I am not good enough. What you have learned in this book is that you are good enough, your strengths will be there to help others in the best ways you know how. There will come a time when you will have the opportunity to help someone else.

Accepting help with grace means you are letting someone else experience the joy of giving.

Accepting with gratitude says, I may never be able to repay you or thank you enough and you are appreciated.

We have covered a lot of information in a short amount of time. Remember to start small. Take one chapter, one paragraph, one word at a time to start making a difference in your life.

I pray you will find the person you were always meant to be. I love you because you are worth it.

4 Reasons Why Asking for Help Makes You a Stronger, Not Weaker, Leader

David Stuart and Todd Nordstrom, Former Contributor for Forbes

- You've chosen to live in a discomfort zone. This is the first thing you need to understand if you're in a position where you need to ask for help—the fact that you're working in a zone that is forcing you to grow and develop. That's a good thing. If you were living and working in a comfort zone, you're not changing for the better. In fact, in a recent New York Times interview, Barstool Sports CEO said, "Any young person should, at some point, take a job that makes them uncomfortable and that they feel unqualified for. It's really great to feel uncomfortable, and you change so much as a person from that."

- You've chosen to protect your greatest asset. This is the second thing you need to understand if you're in a position of asking for help—you will eventually break yourself if you take on too much. The fact that you know you need help is a protective measure—you can only take on so many tasks, and you can only consume so much information. In fact, a LexisNexis survey of 1,700 professionals in the U.S., China, South Africa, the U.K. and Australia showed that typical "employees spend more than half their workdays receiving and managing information rather than using it to do their job." And 50% of those workers reported that they were "reaching a breaking point." You need to keep you intact.

- You gain different and varying insights. This one totally flips the idea that asking for help makes you look weak. The Great Work Study, conducted by the O.C. Tanner Institute, showed that 72% of people who received awards for their work ask for advice, help, insights, and opinions from people outside of their inner circle. In doing so, those workers generate fresh ideas and perspectives on how to solve problems that they otherwise wouldn't have imagined. In essence, asking for help and advice creates better, stronger, more successful results than not asking for help.

- You're building the people around you. We often write and talk about the power of appreciation. And although you may not have considered it before, asking for help is a way to show people that you trust their ideas, feel competent in their skills, and cherish their advice. Ask your team for input. Ask them for ideas. Just like real estate, or stocks, or fine art appreciates with time and influence, you have the power to appreciate the value of the people who surround you. Yes, recognize someone's talent and skill can come on the form of asking for help.

APPENDIX

On the next pages, you will find a list of values and instructions for determining what is important to you.

If there is something missing, feel free to add it.

Accountability
Accuracy
Achievement
Adventurousness
Altruism
Ambition
Assertiveness
Balance
Being the best
Belonging
Boldness
Calmness
Carefulness
Challenge
Cheerfulness
Clear-mindedness
Commitment
Community
Compassion
Competitiveness
Consistency
Contentment
Continuous Improvement
Contribution
Control
Cooperation
Correctness
Courtesy
Courage
Creativity

Diligence
Discipline
Discretion
Diversity
Dynamism
Economy
Effectiveness
Efficiency
Elegance
Empathy
Enjoyment
Enthusiasm
Equality
Excitement
Expertise
Exploration
Expressiveness
Fairness
Faith
Family
Fidelity
Fitness
Fluency
Focus
Freedom
Fun
Generosity
Goodness
Grace
Growth
Happiness
Hard Work
Health

Humility
Independence
Ingenuity
Inner Harmony
Inquisitiveness
Insightfulness
Integrity
Intelligence
Intellectual Status
Intuition
Joy
Justice
Leadership
Legacy
Love
Loyalty
Making a difference
Mastery
Merit
Obedience
Openness
Order
Originality
Patriotism
Perfection
Piety
Positivity
Practicality
Preparedness

Rigor
Security
Self-actualization
Self-control
Selflessness
Self-reliance
Sensitivity
Serenity
Service
Shrewdness
Simplicity
Soundness
Speed
Spontaneity
Stability
Strategic
Strength
Structure
Success
Support
Teamwork
Temperance
Thankfulness
Thoroughness
Thoughtfulness
Timeliness
Tolerance
Traditionalism
Trustworthiness

Curiosity	Helping	Professionalis	Truth-seeking
Decisiveness	Society	m	Understandin
Democraticnes	Holiness	Prudence	g
s	Honesty	Quality	Uniqueness
Dependability	Honor	Reliability	Unity
Determination		Resourcefuln	Usefulness
Devoutness		ess	Vision
		Restraint	Vitality
		Results	

Example:

1) Write down or highlight the values that stick out to you:

Accountability	Balance	Calmness
Carefulness	Health	Courage
Integrity	Community	Freedom
Family	Empathy	Faith
Spirituality	Fun	Support

2) Group your values; no more than five groups:

3) Chose one word from each column to represent the

Freedom	Community	Courage
Faith	Family	Integrity
Balance	Support	Carefulness
Health	Empathy	Accountability
Calmness	Fun	
Spirituality		

values you have listed:

Faith	Family	Integrity

4) Why are these core values important to me?

EPILOGUE

Loving Me is Easy

Recap to help you on your journey.

Congratulations for making a choice. The decisions you make for yourself from here on out will help lead you to your best life full of joy, happiness, belonging and success. I am so excited for this chapter! Everything in my life has brought me to this point. Now I have had the joy to share with you the path that has led me to the happiest, most fulfilling life I could have ever imagined.

You have unlimited potential. Believe it. You are an amazing human being. Live it! You love with your whole heart. Embrace it! Only you can be the leader of your life. Take back your power, find your voice and use it to lead whole-heartedly.

We have covered a lot in this short book. The stories I have shared with you are just a few that have had an impact on my life. Trust me when I say there are a lot more. I hope you take to heart the lessons I have learned.

In the wonder years I made a lot of poor choices. I hated the person I had become. Now we know that everything happens for a reason. This book is for you. You are enough. You can find peace, joy, happiness and success not regardless of your past but because of it.

At the end of this book you will find a list of books and resources. Some of the books are dry but trust me when I say they are worth reading. These books have been my mentors when I didn't have the courage to ask for help when I needed it most.

Here is what I hope you have taken away from this book.:

- Living in your integrity will change your life for the better almost immediately.
- You are just as perfect as every human being on this planet.
- Shame and blame are the catalysts for destroying your self-worth. Talk about it.
- Self-pity and pity parties derail your goal in building solid relationships.
- Mistakes are just decisions where you didn't like the outcome.
- Friends can help you across the bridge if you are willing to listen.

- Your words have power. What you say and believe is what you will attract in your life.
- Personal responsibility is the path to creating your best life.
- Feelings and emotions are human nature. Don't bottle them up and wait for the explosion.
- Accept what is. You cannot change the past.
- You made choices and decisions based on the information you had and what you wanted at the time.
- Vulnerability is a strength not a weakness.
- You don't have to fit in to belong. Authenticity is being honest and showing up.
- Trust yourself. Your intuitive mind will help guide you through the process of finding your own self-love.
- No one has the right to lead your life but you.
- Whole-hearted leadership is CLEAR.
- Relationships are built on trust, respect and communication.
- Self-care, and self-love are not selfish but are critical in living your best life.

Everything happens for a reason. God knows your mistakes before you do and He has a plan.

In 2020, I made a decision to leave a long-standing career so I could help others learn how to trust and believe in themselves. Today, I am a very happy, successful author, speaker, trainer and coach. I didn't believe I would ever own my own home or a reliable car let alone start my own business.

I have hired several coaches to help declutter my brain. I have read tons of books to design my future and continue working on personal growth to develop my life and lead on my terms.

Since 2020, I have consulted business owners on how to grow their teams, retain employees, communicate, and build trust with their leaders.

I have coached individuals to become the best version of themselves. Through a 3-step program to declutter, design and develop their own path.

I have worked with parents to help them communicate with their tweens and teens and build strong relationships.

I have created workshops for tweens and teens to help them grow and learn how to navigate their world with confidence.

Most importantly I have built relationships with my own children, my spouse and my friends.

I have found that sense of belonging I didn't know I was looking for.

Notes

Introduction

Maxwell, J. (2012). *15 Invaluable Laws of Growth.* New York: Center Street.

The Truth Behind the Wolf Pack

Maxwell, J (2015). *The Leadership Handbook: 26 Critical Lessons Every Leader Needs.* Nashville: Nelson Books.

Chapter 1

Wake Forest University definition of emotions and feelings.

Brown, B. (2015). *Rising Strong: The Reckoning. The Rumble. The Revolution.* New York: Random House.

Brown, B. (2012). *Daring Greatly: How the Courage to Be Vulnerable Transforms the Way We Live, Love, Parent, and Lead.* New York: Avery.

Maraboli, S. (2013). *Unapologetically You: Reflections on Life and the Human Experience.* USA: Author.

Tangney, J., Dearing, R. Retrieved from https://www.scientificamerican.com/article/the-scientific-underpinnings-and-impacts-of-shame/.

Brown, B. (2018). *Dare to Lead: Brave Work. Tough Conversations. Whole Hearts.* New York: Random House.

Chapter 2

Battistelli, F. (2008). "Behind the Scenes." On *My Paper Heart*, track nine. Word Entertainment LLC.

Douglas, K. (1988). *The Ragman's Son.* New York: Simon and Schuster.

Brown, B. (2015). *Rising Strong: The Reckoning. The Rumble. The Revolution.* New York: Random House Publishing.

Wilson, C. (2021). What is Self-Sabotage? How to Help Stop the Vicious Cycle. *Journal of Sabotage.* 201-206. Retrieved from https://positivepsychology.com/self-sabotage.

Duval & Wicklund. (1972). Retrieved from https://www.encyclopedia.com/social-sciences/applied-and-social-sciences-magazines/self-awareness-theory.

Jung, C (1989). *Memories, Dreams, Reflections.* New York: Vintage Books.

Chapter 3

Picoult, J. (2012). *My Sister's Keeper.* New York: Washington Square Press.

Picoult, J. (2012). *My Sister's Keeper*. New York: Washington Square Press.

Picoult, J. (2002). *Salem Falls*. New York: Washington Square Press.

Chapter 4

Shelby, L. (2019). *No Hands, No Excuses: Living a No Excuse Life, No Matter What Happens to You*. USA: Author.

Bradberry, T. Greaves, J. (2009). *Emotional Intelligence 2.0*. San Diego: TalentSmart.

David, S. (2016). *Emotional Agility*. New York: Avery.

Brown, B. (2015). *Daring Greatly: How the Courage to Be Vulnerable Transforms the Way We Live, Love, Parent, and Lead*. New York: Avery.

Brown, B. (2021). *Atlas of the Heart: Mapping Meaningful Connection and the Language of Human Experience*. New York: Random House.

Chapter 5

Fitzmaurice, S. Retrieved from https://www.goodreads.com/author/quotes/4207373.Sue_Fitzmaurice.

Brown, B. (2010). *The Gifts of Imperfection*. Center City: Hazelden Publishing.

Maxwell, J. (2012). *15 Invaluable Laws of Growth*. New York: Center Street.

Grant, A. (2014). *Give and Take: Why Helping Others Drive Our Success*. New York: Penguin Books.

Hazelden Betty Ford Foundation. (2018). Boundaries in Addiction Recovery: What is a Boundary?. Retrieved from https://www.hazeldenbettyford.org/articles/boundaries-in-addiction-recovery.

Lerner, R. (2009). *The Object of My Affection Is in My Reflection: Coping with Narcissists*. Deerfield Beach: Health Communication Inc.

Duke, P. (1992). *A Brilliant Madness: Living with Manic-Depressive Illness*. New York: Bantam Books.

Chapter 6

Ziglar, Z. (2014). Retrieved from https://www.facebook.com/ZigZiglar/posts/when-you-focus-on-problems-you-get-more-problems-when-you-focus-on-possibilities/10152487493787863.

Maxwell, J. (2022). What is C.L.E.A.R.? Retrieved from https://www.johnmaxwellacademy.com/c-l-e-a-r.

Brown, B. (2012). *Daring Greatly: How the Courage to Be Vulnerable Transforms the Way We Live, Love, Parent, and Lead*. New York: Avery.

Brown, B. (2015). *Rising Strong: The Reckoning. The Rumble. The Revolution*. New York: Spiegel and Grau.

Chapter 7

Brown, B. (2018). *Dare to Lead: Brave Work. Tough Conversations. Whole Hearts.* New York: Random House.

Clear, J. (2018). *Atomic Habits: An Easy & Proven Way to Build Good Habits & Break Bad Ones.* New York: Avery.

Stone, W.C. (2017). *The Success System that Never Fails.* Blacksburg: Wilder Publications.

Reilly, C. (2019). *Unleash Your Inner Voice: An Introvert's Guide to Overcoming the Itty-Bitty Shitty Committee.* Shine Publishing House

Ball, Z. (2022). Retrieved from https://www.brainyquote.com/quotes/zoe_ball_1191699.

Chapter 8

Gide, A. (2021). *The Journals of André Gide: 1889-1949.* Hassell Street Press.

Warrell, M. (2021). *Stop Playing Safe: How to Be Braver in Your Work, Leadership, and Life.* Milton: John Wiley & Sons Australia Ltd.

Chapman, G. (2015). *The Five Love Languages: The Secret to Love That Lasts.* Chicago: Northfield Publishing.

Stuart, D., Nordstrom, T. (2017). Retrieved from https://www.forbes.com/sites/davidsturt/2017/11/01/4-reasons-why-asking-for-help-makes-you-a-stronger-not-weaker-leader/?sh=34d53aff3c1a.

LAURIE'S LIST

The following collection of books and courses have shaped my growth and understanding how to love others and love myself. (Listed alphabetically by author's last name)

Aksamit, Scott: *Emotional Self Defense*

Brown, Brené: *Dare to Lead*
The Gifts of Imperfection
Atlas of the Heart
Daring Greatly
Rising Strong
Braving the Wilderness

Bradberry, Travis &
Jean Greaves: *Emotional Intelligence 2.0*

Clear, James: *Atomic Habits*

Covey, Steven: *7 Habits of Highly Effective People*

David, Susan: *Emotional Agility*

Maxwell, John: *15 Invaluable Laws of Growth*
Everyone Communicates, Few Connect
Put Your Dreams to the Test
21 Irrefutable Laws of Leadership
Leadership Gold

Becoming a Person of Influence

Natzke, Chris: *Black Belt Leadership*

Raymond, Vanessa: *Killer Confidence*

Reilly, Cathy: *Unleash Your Inner Voice*

Riccoti, Sonia: *Bounce Back System (Lead Out Loud),* online

Silva, Jose: *The Silva Method of Mind Control*

ABOUT THE AUTHOR

Laurie Kroeger

Author, Trainer, Speaker, and Coach.

I was raised with three sets of parents. I always felt loved, but I never felt like I really belonged. It wasn't until I learned to love who I am because of my mistakes that I found true belonging, happiness, and peace in my life. Trusting in who I am and the decisions I've made helped me to overcome the shame and regret that stole so much of my life, created many doubts, and lowered my self-confidence. I have spent the last 22 years on a journey to understand me.

After decades of bad decision making, I am here to share with you how I moved from pain and despair to self-love and success. From never believing I would amount to anything to owning a coaching and consulting business and a nonprofit camp for tweens and teens in the works. I have three beautiful, amazing children, 4 grandchildren and a husband of 9 years who loves and supports me in all of my crazy journeys.

I hope that you will step out of your comfort zone and become the person I know you were meant to be.

If you have more questions than answers, you are on the right track. It means you have reignited your curiosity.

If you would like to explore options for:

- 1:1 coaching – free 30-minute discovery session.
- Business consulting – lunch 'n' learns, masterminds, growth workshops and more.
- Leadership or communication training – Certified John Maxwell programs, C.L.E.A.R strategies.

Contact:

support@VisiblePotential.com

If you would like to have Laurie Kroeger as a speaker, email:

Laurie@visiblepotential.com

For more information about upcoming events Laurie will be conducting, visit:

LovingMeisHard.com

For information visit: www.visiblepotential.com

Made in the USA
Columbia, SC
20 February 2023

12615609R00089